Archaeology

Blishen Books

edited by Edward Blishen

Other titles:
Cooking
Making Music
Modern Puppetry
Tape Recording
Natural History
Collecting
Fishing

Archaeology

Jim Ingram

Michael Joseph, London

First published in Great Britain by
MICHAEL JOSEPH LTD
26 *Bloomsbury Street*
London, W.C.1
1969

Illustrated by Graham Humphreys
Designed by M. Mohan

7181 0673 3

Set and printed in Great Britain by Tonbridge Printers Ltd, Peach Hall Works, Tonbridge, Kent, in Garamond eleven on thirteen point, and bound by James Burn at Esher, Surrey

Contents

Acknowledgements

The author wishes to thank the numerous archaeologists, amateur and professional, whose advice and skills have contributed to the writing of this book. Special thanks go to Mr Raymond Hayes, M.B.E. of Hutton-le-Hole, Yorkshire, fellow-worker in the field of amateur archaeology for twenty-five joyous years, and to the late Dr Philip Corder, of the Society of Antiquaries, for the kindly way in which he was prepared to share his knowledge of archaeology with inexperienced beginners.

The writer also wishes to thank the various persons and organisations who kindly provided information and illustrations; among them the Coalbrookdale Company Ltd., the Ministry of Public Building and Works, and the Controller of Her Majesty's Stationery Office.

He also wishes to thank Dr. Glyn Daniel and the Editor of *The Listener* for permission to make use of the quotation on page 63.

About This Book

First of all – let us rid ourselves of two mistaken ideas about archaeology:

(1) You don't have to do any digging to be an archaeologist.

(2) Archaeology isn't just concerned with people and happenings of long ago, or in prehistoric times. It deals also with quite recent events, things that happened in your own lifetime or that of your family.

Let us examine these two statements more closely.

Digging things up. Certainly much archaeological knowledge has been gained by excavation, and it is useful to have some personal knowledge of a 'dig'; but even if you have never handled a spade or a pick in your life, you can still do useful work and have great enjoyment from undertaking archaeological field-work. This requires little more than a measuring-tape and note-book, a metal probing-rod, a stout pair of boots and some know-how. More about this later.

Long, long ago. Some books about archaeology give a reader the impression that only matters relating to prehistoric times, or at least to the Roman and medieval periods, can be classed as archaeology. This isn't so. Archaeology is concerned with all man's activities in the past. And the past began only yesterday.

So archaeological investigation doesn't stop with Iron Age forts or Roman villas or old castles. It includes remains from the 19th and 20th centuries as well – such objects as railway locomotives, canal boats, motor cars and steam-engines. These things are also the concern of the archaeologist, since they are *artifacts* (that is, objects made by human beings) to be studied in the same way that we study flint arrow-heads to learn about the Stone Age. They are all part of the story of man's technological development.

Archaeological investigation doesn't stop at some arbitrarily determined point in time. It goes on.

The first space ships launched in the 1950s (which I saw in Moscow a year or so ago) are now archaeological exhibits. Tramcars, a familiar sight on city streets only ten or fifteen years ago, can be examined only in museums. Steam trains have almost vanished from the British landscape. Early 20th-century motor cars would have disappeared, too, but for the efforts of devoted groups of enthusiasts.

The world around us disintegrates and vanishes almost without our being aware of it. There's work to be done, if all this is not to pass unrecorded.

That's the fascination of archaeology. You can do something about it yourself – as an amateur. I use the word in the sense of one who pursues a study from a natural love of finding out. If you are interested in the past you can't travel anywhere in the British Isles without discovering something of interest – prehistoric, Roman, medieval, modern. It is just a matter of knowing what to look for. The aim of this book is to help you to acquire that knowledge.

Archaeology as a hobby has developed during the past decade. Television programmes have roused the interest of millions of people who might otherwise never have discovered how fascinating it is. And dozens of 'digs' take place every year at which beginners can acquire the necessary practical experience.

Probably few readers of this book will become professional archaeologists. But there is nothing to stop anyone from becoming a part-time archaeologist. Once you have developed a real grasp and love of the subject it is capable of keeping you occupied for the rest of your life because, like exploration or detective work (both of which it resembles), it never comes to an end. Solving problems is the essence of all three activities, and most of us fancy pitting our wits against something puzzling – even if we don't always succeed.

This book will not make you into an archaeologist – only you can do that. But it will help you to get started.

What is Archaeology?

At St Albans, in Hertfordshire, ninety young people have been excavating part of the Belgic settlement which existed before the Roman city. The Belgae were a Celtic people who migrated to this district from the Continent before Christ was born. The reason for the excavation was to discover more about their civilization. The ninety amateur archaeologists, with their shovels and trowels, played an important part in this investigation.

If you go to Crich, in Derbyshire, you will see a group of people, dressed in blue overalls, repairing and painting old tram-cars, and then testing them by running them along a length of track laid down inside an old quarry. This is the Tramway Museum, where the biggest collection of old tramcars in the country has been brought together by a group of enthusiasts determined that examples of this once-familiar form of transport should be preserved before it is too late.

Not long ago I stood in a muddy trench somewhere in London while an enthusiastic young archaeologist pointed out the remains of a Roman boat exposed in a silted-up creek by the River Thames. He was a member of the Southwark Archaeological Excavation Committee which is concerned with discovering what life was like on the south bank of the Thames in Roman and later times.

Anyone who has watched archaeologists at work has probably asked himself such questions as: What is archaeology? What do archaeologists do? How do they do it? And finally, *Why* do they do it?

Let's consider the first question. Archaeology has been defined in various ways. Perhaps the best puts it like this: that archaeology is the term applied to the study of the material remains of past ages, whether they are buildings or the ruins of buildings, above or below ground, or objects in daily use such as coins, pottery, tools, weapons, machinery or industrial workings.

This definition, in fact, covers everything constructed or established by man in his efforts to maintain life on earth.

Among the buildings that it includes (whether they are in ruins or are still lived and worked in) are sacred structures such as temples, burial mounds, graves. It also includes fortified places such as earthworks, castles, forts: roads and trackways: quarries and gravel-pits: clothing, weapons, armour. Then there are things used to make other things – in spinning, weaving, farming, gardening, carpentry, metal-working, masonry: the first machines, ships, other forms of transport.

Anything a man makes is a reflection of his way of living, and of the society in which he lives. Therefore almost every 'find' can tell us something about the life of the people who used it. Though written records may not exist, such remains provide clues to past ways of living.

One fact ought never to be forgotten – that archaeologists do not study old things only for the sake of the things themselves, but also for what these can tell us about *people*. It is the *people* who matter, more than the objects. It's easy to forget an obvious truth – that people of the past, no matter how long ago they lived, and whether in ancient Egypt, Palestine, India or America, were very much the same as us, with the same emotions, loves, fears, hatreds. And behind every object that's the concern of archaeology –

every castle, flint arrow-head or iron sword – there's a human story.

Most of us are interested in other people – how they lived. The problems which faced them are the same problems that face us now – getting an education or a living, getting on with other people, including those we don't like and those who have power over us. These problems haven't changed, even if material circumstances have. Archaeology enables us to enter into the lives of people, very much like ourselves, who happened to live at earlier periods of history.

The answer to that second question, about what archaeologists do, is a very simple one. They seek, in many different ways, to find out how people lived in the past. But how do they do it?

Of course, they dig. They excavate the sites of settlements and workings and they plot out the distribution of such sites on maps. On such maps, finds of coins, pottery, weapons and tools are also recorded. And from the facts contained in the maps, and from published reports of excavations and field work, a synthesis (a drawing together) of new knowledge can be built up.

Sometimes the remains dug up by archaeologists are fairly complete, as was the Saxon royal ship-burial at Sutton Hoo, in Suffolk. (These marvellous finds can be seen in the British Museum). Sometimes the remains are fragmentary, no more than the 'ghost' of a body or of an object that has almost disappeared. In either case, modern archaeological skills and techniques can extract the utmost amount of information. Such finds are particularly important when they throw light on periods of which there are no written records.

Much of the more recent past can be reconstructed or illustrated from written documents of the time, but even these, by themselves, can't illuminate the daily life of the ordinary man so well as a handful of objects found during a well-conducted archaeological excavation.

But however carefully a site is excavated, and however good a picture of the life of our ancestors is pieced together by that means, there remains much that we can only guess at. We still may find it difficult to know how they *thought* – what their religious and political beliefs were, their social organisation, the ways in which they solved the problems of their day. Only where there are written records does this task become easier.

Finally: Why do archaeologists do what they do? Why study archaeology at all?

The simplest answer is that any nation that calls itself civilised has a duty to preserve the records of its past life, and to ensure that the achievements of its ancestors, in so far as they remain or are to be discovered, are not destroyed.

Nearly all peoples are interested in their own past. Primitive people, who have no historical records and no archaeology, satisfy this curiosity by constructing myths and legends about their ancestors. But civilised people require something more exact and scientific.

I remember the late Professor Gordon Childe explaining it to a group of us – describing to us the whole impulse behind archaeology – at the end of a lecture. During the past 5,000 years, he said, civilisations in various parts of the earth had kept records in which was contained their knowledge of the world around them. Only a part of this knowledge has come down to us people of the 20th century, in books and manuscripts which have been repeatedly copied or reprinted. The rest has to be recovered from the wreckage of the past, sometimes of vanished civilisations. Archaeology began when men started systematically to hunt for the facts of human knowledge that were not contained in old manuscripts.

Geoffrey Bibby has said it well in a book called *The Testimony of the Spade:*

'Every archaeologist knows in his heart why he digs. He digs, in pity and humility, that the dead may live again, that something may be salvaged from the wrack of ages, that the past may colour the present and give heart to the future. His excavations are the only payment we can make against the debt we owe to those who, through the millenia, fashioned the earth on which we live.'

How to get Started

Archaeology is a hobby you can follow, and take part in, at various levels depending on your degree of knowledge and the extent to which you are willing to become involved.

At the simplest level, archaeology is a matter of visiting ancient monuments and speculating about the lives of the people who built them. An ancient monument can be anything from a prehistoric stone circle to a Roman fort or a medieval manor-house. There are thousands of these in the British Isles, carefully preserved by such organizations as the National Trust and the Ministry of Works. The only skill needed in this form of archaeology is the ability to reach such monuments; they are there waiting to be looked at. This is a purely *visual* aspect of archaeology, a matter of simply looking, and it can give you a great deal of pleasure. You also do learn some archaeology.

The second stage in becoming an archaeologist begins when you take a more active part. There are several ways of doing this: either by going on field-trips organized by a society, or by helping to excavate a site about which little is known – prehistoric, Roman, medieval, or later. This experience helps to deepen your knowledge, as well as giving the pleasure which comes from doing a worthwhile job.

The third stage is when, probably with a few fellow-workers, you start to do field-work by yourselves. You now begin to feel that you are a real archaeologist.

Finally you may want to become really involved, and go to university to study for a degree or diploma in archaeology. Eventually you may decide to make it a full-time occupation, and become a supervisor, director, or curator of a museum. But not many amateurs are able to do that.

There are other ways of becoming an archaeologist – by-ways, you might call them. I knew a man who began his archaeological career as a 'beachcomber',

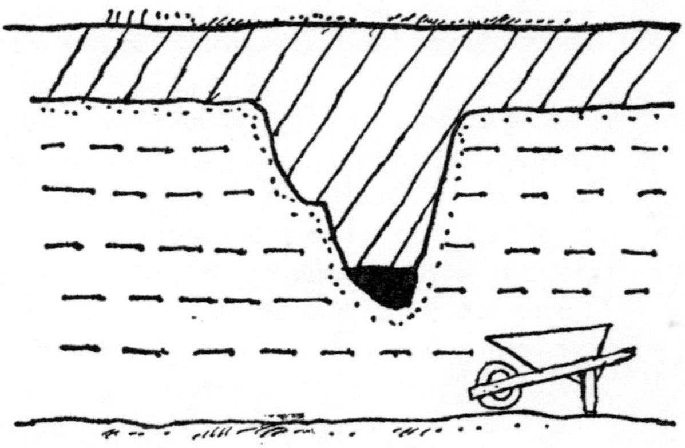

Cross-section of gravel pit, showing cavity which may be ancient ditch or storage pit

looking for objects which had somehow got lost in the mudbanks along the River Thames. He collected clay pipes, coins, pottery, footwear, small finds. When last I heard of him he had collected enough finds to start a museum.

But how can *you* get started?

You have, let us say, a feeling for the past, you are stirred by the sight of old things – whether they are earthworks, buildings, roads, machines, transport – but you have little knowledge and few chances of learning. What then?

Archaeology is largely a local study. In whichever part of the British Isles you may happen to live there are bound to be objects of archaeological interest, if you care to go and find them. There is no need to travel far. You can start where you are. Many of us have carried on our field-work by bicycle, or on foot.

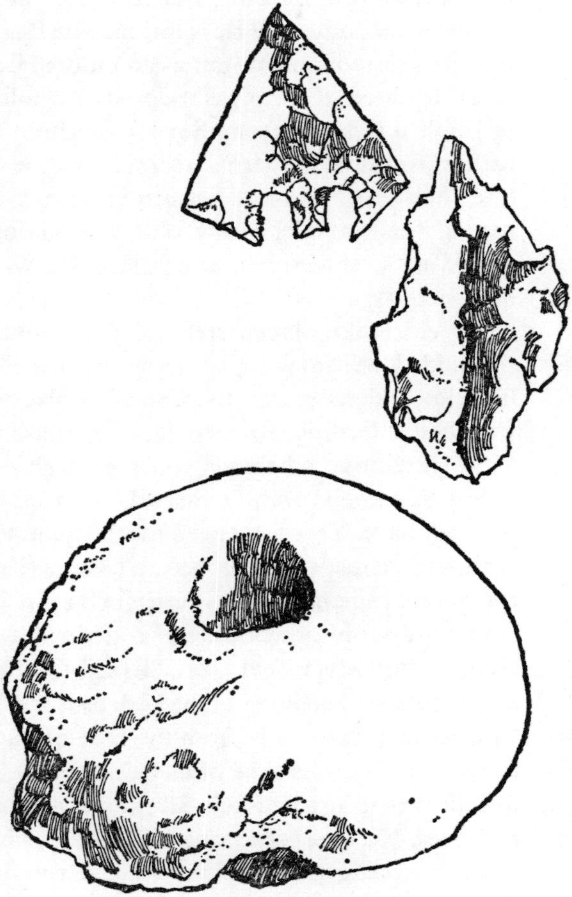

Small Finds – Arrow head, flint borer, pre-Roman quern for grinding corn

Public transport got us to other sites. A bicycle has the advantage that it can be ridden along old tracks, or carried over rough country, if need be.

It's no excuse to say you live in a big industrial

centre, which contains little that is old or exciting. No part of Britain is dull if you are historically-minded. Places such as Manchester or Birmingham may not have prehistoric remains, but they are full of monuments of the Industrial Revolution. The Black Country may be grim to look at, but as an industrial museum it is unsurpassed, showing as it does the whole evolution of English Industry from the palaeotechnic (that is, the earliest forms of modern machinery) to the neotechnic (the latest forms). Among many remarkable monuments, for example, is the oldest surviving Boulton and Watt steam-engine, which stopped work only a few years ago.

Big cities like Manchester and Birmingham possess the added advantage that they usually have better libraries and museums than smaller places, together with better facilities for attending lectures.

So start now, wherever you are. Archaeology is a hobby that can be usefully carried out in any spare time you may have. You don't need much equipment to start with – some maps, a notebook, a camera (I've found a cheap box camera useful) – not much more.

For years my notebook has contained a maxim of General Pitt-Rivers, who established the foundations of scientific archaeology in the 19th century. He wrote: 'A discovery dates only from the time of the record of it, and not from the time of its being found.' I've tried to follow that instruction in all my own archaeological activities. No observation or field-work or indeed any kind of investigation is of any value if you don't write down what you have seen and done. As time passes, one forgets.

So keep a record, even if it is only a cheap note-book with a few dates and details, a sketch-map or two, and some picture postcards and photographs. You'll find it of great value later on. I have a shelf full of just such notebooks. At most sites booklets are sold that tell the history of the place, with plans and pictures, and this is a cheap way of gaining concise technical information. Collect these also.

What you can do now. There are a number of things you can do immediately.

1. Join a local archaeological society.
2. Attend any lectures arranged locally by such organisations as the Workers' Educational Association, or by the nearest university.
3. Read as many books about archaeology as you can.
4. Visit as many archaeological sites as possible.
5. Visit museums and examine their contents.
6. Get some experience of field-archaeology.
7. Join a 'dig' for experience of large-scale excavation.

All these activities will be dealt with in the succeeding chapters of this book. Meanwhile, let us consider some of them in more detail.

1. *Joining a society.* You can find out whether there is an archaeological society in your neighbourhood by asking at the public library. By joining the right kind of society you'll be able to add to your knowledge without delay. However, such organisations do vary in quality.

The larger and well-organised societies may offer such facilities as libraries, where books difficult to obtain are available, and perhaps a museum. Often they organise excavations and field-trips. Membership at a reduced fee is usually possible if you are under twenty-one.

Such societies may run lecture courses where members can hear well-known archaeologists discuss technical aspects of the subject. The societies may be linked with a local university and be the source of much local archaeological activity. They may publish volumes of *Transactions* in which is recorded the work carried on by members, or at least a news-sheet. All this the beginner will find valuable, if only for the sake of contact with better-informed people.

Smaller societies may be less well-organised, and their activities may consist only of a few outings or meetings. In any case, it is worthwhile to join.

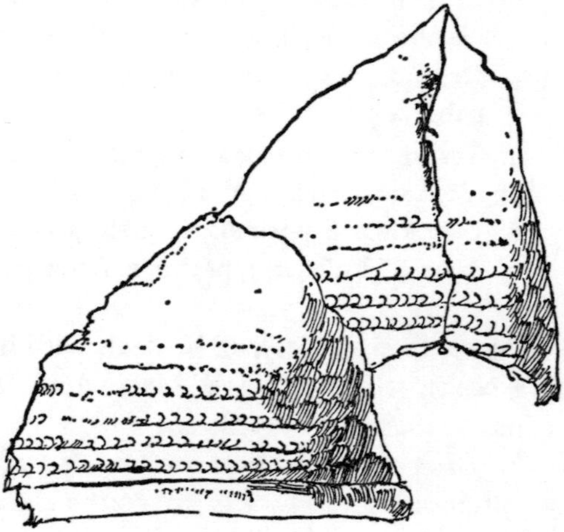

Fragment of early pottery known as 'Beaker Ware'

There are also the national societies, such as the British Archaeological Institute, but they are not of great concern to the beginner.

2. *Attending lectures.* Courses of lectures are often organised by the extramural departments of universities or by the Workers' Educational Association. So much has the subject developed during recent years that there are now specialised courses dealing with different periods – prehistoric, Roman, medieval and so on. As well as general courses in Industrial Archaeology there are others that deal with the development of railways, canals, transport or industry. Field-trips are often arranged in connection with such lectures.

These organisations also often conduct summer schools, where you can spend a week or more attending lectures and going on excursions.

3. *Visiting sites.* A knowledge of the different types of archaeological monument – burial mounds, stone circles, forts, Roman remains and so on – is a necessary part of the archaeologist's equipment. So visit as many of these sites as possible so that you know what they look like. Fortunately the task has been made easy for us, since 9,000 sites have been scheduled for preservation by the Ministry of Works. There can hardly be any part of the country which is without a number of examples. (More details are given in the next chapter). From looking at what has already been identified you can sharpen your power to recognise the site as yet undiscovered. It is one thing to identify a prehistoric tomb that has been neatly cleared out and made accessible, but quite another matter when you have to locate a similar structure that may be half-buried among rocks and overgrown with trees and bushes.

4. *Reading about archaeology.* This is a subject on its own, and is dealt with at length later in the book.

5. *Visit museums.* Just as you need to visit ancient monuments in order to learn to recognise *structures,* so you must be able to identify objects of the kind that have been found inside these structures. Tools and weapons of stone, bronze and iron, objects in daily use in Roman or medieval times – *see,* and if possible *handle,* as many different things of this sort as you can. You'll then find it easier to recognise similar objects when you encounter them in the muddy confines of an actual excavation. It is in museums that you can build up this vital experience.

My remaining suggestions as to things you can do immediately – the gaining of experience in field-archaeology and large-scale excavation – are dealt with separately in later chapters.

I have left till last one most helpful source of information and advice – the public library. The staffs of these libraries, and I speak from wide experience, are invariably courteous, helpful and willing to go to great trouble to help you get the information you need. Of course, the libraries vary in size and resources, from Manchester's vast collections and wide range of reference departments (or the great London libraries), to the small local branches of the county libraries. Yet even the smallest library is linked through the National Central Library service to the big collections, and can always get you the vital book you need.

Libraries do much more than lend you books or provide books of reference for you to consult. They often have collections of photographs, newspaper cuttings and manuscripts dealing with local history. Often, too, they have contacts with people who possess knowledge that you can tap. Altogether, the libraries are the would-be archaeologist's best friend.

And don't forget people – just plain, everyday, ordinary people. Policemen, postmen, council workmen, farm workers, transport workers, factory hands, garage men – they may not know much about archaeology, and may prefer a pint in a pub to a lecture, but they are often in a position to observe something of archaeological interest – an old road, some curious stonework, a collection of flints or coins – which they will tell you about if you speak to them properly. Any amount of archaeological investigation must have had its origins in casual conversations with men going about their daily work. So don't be afraid to talk – to anybody.

Schoolchildren can be useful, too. I remember when a party of us were excavating a town of the 'Chariot People' in Yorkshire, we were troubled by the activities of some boys from a local secondary modern school. They shouted at us, and jeered and threw stones. At last, in desperation, we got the two ringleaders, showed them what we were doing, and invited them to help us. After that we had no more trouble, for these two big tough lads made themselves into the guardians of the site, and kept the rest of the crowd in order. And with their sharp eyes they spotted bits of pottery and small coins we had overlooked.

See for Yourself

The amateur archaeologist's first instinct is to get out-of-doors and discover something exciting – a prehistoric tomb or temple, an old castle, a Roman fort. Books can wait until a rainy day!

This is a perfectly reasonable emotion. Follow it. One of the chief delights of archaeology is that it *does* take you out-of-doors – to the moorlands, the mountains, and the seacoast. Every field-trip can be a voyage of discovery – for you. It is *your own* first sight of something old and mysterious – temple or fort or whatever it is – which matters. It is not important that other people have seen it before you. Once seen, the associations of that sight are part of your experience for ever.

I've used the phrase 'ancient monument'. It crops up frequently in archaeology, so we'd better be clear what it means. An ancient monument is anything that has survived from the past. Generally the term is applied to structures – things on the ground such as walls, buildings, stones, graves – but it can also be applied to written records, inscriptions. 'Ancient monuments' are the concern of the archaeologist, so learn to recognize as many as you can.

Observing old earthworks, buildings, fortifications, settlement sites, is one of the first stages in acquiring a knowledge of archaeology. Personal observation of such things gives you some idea of the way people of any past period actually lived: the people of the Old Stone Age, the New Stone Age, the Bronze and Iron Ages (these are archaeologists' labels for races whose names we will never know); the people of whom there survive written records – the Romans, the Anglo-Saxons, the Danes and Norsemen, the Normans. They all lived in Britain, and all left evidence of their occupation.

So get out of doors and discover what sorts of monuments created by these different races remain in Britain to be investigated. They number thousands. A lifetime would be too short to visit them all. It's of the first importance to know about the key sites, those monuments that are outstanding examples of their kind. Stonehenge and Avebury, for example, are our two finest stone circles, though there are many other less splendid ones. Our finest Stone Age fort is Maiden Castle, in Dorset – though again there are dozens of other examples. It isn't necessary to visit *every* stone circle or hill-fort, but very important to see the outstanding ones.

You need, in these first archaeological travels of yours, to build up such an experience that you know the answers to questions such as the following:

What did a Bronze Age tomb look like? Or a Roman house? Or a Viking settlement? What was the appearance of a walled town of the Middle Ages? Or of an 18th century battleship?

Examples of all these – towns, ships, houses – have been preserved or, on the basis of archaeological investigation, have been reconstructed. Go and see them, as a beginning.

That is how I started myself.

Journey into History. The earliest peoples who lived in Britain left little for us to look at. I don't intend to describe the activities of the hunters and fishermen and food-gatherers of the Old Stone Age – there is a number of excellent books that deal with them. You can, if it pleases you (and I've had much pleasure from it myself), visit caves and rock-shelters in various parts of the country, where evidence of their existence has been found. Nana's Cave, on Caldey Island, off the coast of Pembrokeshire, is one. In the little limestone gorge at Creswell Crags, in Nottinghamshire, are several caves where carved stone objects have been found. The atmosphere of a prehistoric inhabited cave survives in Kent's Cavern, in Torquay, despite the electric lighting that has been installed; and in Yorkshire, Somerset, North and South Wales, there are other caves with evidence of prehistoric occupation.

The limestone uplands were always a favourite home of prehistoric peoples, and many types of remains are found there.

It is often the most spectacular ancient monuments that attract us – the big stone circles, the huge isolated standing stones, the great burial mounds. These objects by their sheer size set our imaginations on fire, and provoke questions. How were such immense stones placed in position? How much manpower was needed? Who was the ruler who, thousands of years ago, had such authority that he could organise the construction of such complicated structures? Archaeologists have worked out answers to some of the technical questions, but other questions – how the people lived and were ruled – remain unanswered.

Some of our greatest prehistoric monuments were the work of the various races whom archaeologists have grouped together under the label of the New Stone and the Bronze Ages. Examples are to be found in almost every part of the British Isles, from the Orkneys to the Isles of Scilly.

Of them all, Stonehenge is certainly the masterwork. It is visited every year by more than a quarter of a million people. This huge stone circle on Salisbury Plain, in Wiltshire, was a temple; but (in the words of the Junior Guide, *What is Stonehenge?*, published by the Ministry of Public Building and Works) 'we shall probably never know what kinds of gods were worshipped by its builders, or what kind of ceremonies took place inside it. Some people have suggested that it was a temple for sun-worship, because the entrance points down the middle towards the sunrise on Midsummer Day, the longest day of the year. This may be true, but it cannot be proved for certain.'

Equally spectacular, though in a different way, is the stone circle at Avebury, less than twenty miles to the north of Stonehenge. Among the relics in the Avebury museum are a pair of rusted medieval tailor's scissors, found on a skeleton crushed under one of the great stones. The story behind *that* is clear enough. Some time in the Middle Ages a number of local people must have tried to displace the great stone (which was probably a hindrance to a local farmer in his ploughing) and the poor tailor was unable to get out of the way in time when it toppled out of control.

There are a number of other big stone circles, and numerous smaller ones. It is interesting work, in moorland or mountain country, searching for lesser-known circles that are now overgrown with vegetation.

On the Mainland island of Orkney is the 'Ring of Brogar', a magnificent megalithic monument, consisting of twenty-seven upright stones each ten to fifteen feet high. ('Megalith' is the technical name given to any huge prehistoric stone). Another fine circle can be seen in a field at Keswick, in the Lake District.

Ancient circles are things to wonder at and puzzle over – but so are the immense solitary stone monoliths that are to be found in many places. ('Monolith' means a single stone). The tallest stone of this kind in Britain is the Rudstone, which crowns a hilltop seven miles from Bridlington, in Yorkshire. It stands nearly twenty-seven feet high, and there is said to be an equal length of stone buried underground. Also in Yorkshire, near Boroughbridge, are the three enormous monoliths known as 'The Devil's Arrows'. Smaller and less startling stones can be found in many places – in Derbyshire, Cornwall, Wales and elsewhere.

The great burial mounds erected by the peoples of prehistory are as astounding as the stone circles,

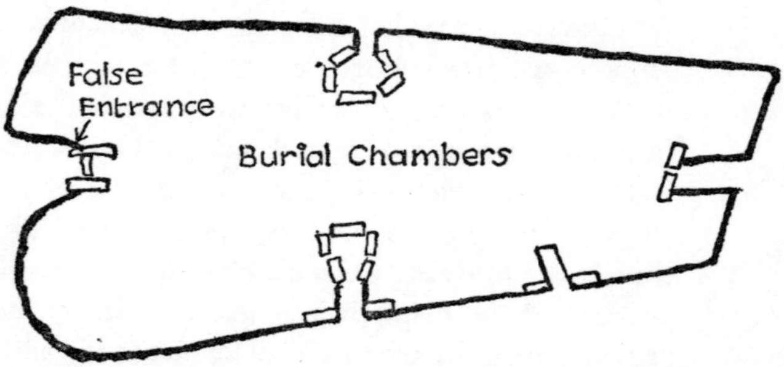

Plan of a Long Barrow, based on Belas Knap, Gloucestershire

though in a different fashion. Big tombs such as La Hougue Bie, on the island of Jersey, Maeshowe on Orkney and Newgrange Tumulus in Ireland, are the equivalent in these islands of the pyramids of Egypt. In them kings and chieftains were buried three or four thousand years ago.

The mound of Maeshowe, on Orkney, is spectacular for the stonework of its central chamber. Carved with sword-points on the walls are inscriptions in the runic alphabet of the Vikings ('runes' being written or carved symbols), telling how a party of them sheltered in the chamber while on their way to Jerusalem. La Hougue Bie had the unhappy fate of being incorporated into the German defences of the island of Jersey during the last war, so that it now displays two periods of archaeology: one thousands of years past, the other a score of years only.

Burial mounds of various types are found in almost every part of Britain. You should inquire locally for any examples there may be (perhaps not very widely known) in your own district.

Less easy to locate than tombs and temples are the house-sites and settlements of these ancient peoples. Here there is much scope for individual investigation. There are some in Cornwall, and others on Dartmoor. One of the best places I know to view a Bronze Age settlement, with its surrounding field-walls, is on the island of Lundy, in the Bristol Channel. It is called Gannets' Coombe, and several houses are in a fair state of preservation. But Lundy is altogether an archaeologist's paradise, with remains stretching from the New Stone Age to 19th century industrialism.

A complete little settlement of New Stone Age Houses has been preserved at Skara Brae, in the Orkneys. The whole settlement was buried under sand dunes for several thousand years. Then, when a storm of exceptional severity blew the sand away, the stone walls of the houses and alleyways of the village were exposed. Everything inside the dwellings was made of stone – beds, tables, cupboards – indicating that the inhabitants had no wood to work with. This is the really remarkable point about that village – ancient articles of furniture, being of perishable wood, are rarely preserved.

Also in Orkney, on the island of Hoy, is one of the most remarkable monuments in the British Isles – a huge block of sandstone called the Dwarfie Stone. The sandstone is hollowed out to form a rock-cut tomb, of a type known in countries bordering on the Mediterranean, but unknown here except in this example, which dates from the late Neolithic or early Bronze Age.

I've mentioned, almost in a breath, places as far apart as the Orkneys, Wiltshire and Ireland. You will find that visiting places of archaeological interest takes you the length and breadth of the British Isles; in fact, you can very well make such visits the basis of your holidays.

The next ancient peoples, in historical order, were those of the Iron Age. These (who first emerge in our history books as the 'Ancient Britons' or 'the Celts') have left many monuments for our investigation. The most spectacular are the hill-forts to be found in many parts of the country. Maiden Castle, near Dorchester in Dorset, is the outstanding example, its massive defences dominating the surrounding countryside. The ramparts were defended by squads of men armed with slings, which were fired from stone platforms. One platform, when the archaeologists got to work on it, was found still to hold its reserve of sling-stones – 20,000 of them!

Somewhere about the year AD 43 or 44 Maiden Castle was stormed and captured by the Second Augustan Legion under the command of the future Emperor, Vespasian. The main attack was against the eastern gate, where a volley of iron-headed ballista-bolts mowed down many of the defenders. The rest were cut down by Roman swords. A war cemetery, the earliest known in Britain, provided evidence of the slaughter during and after the battle.

There are so many hill-forts worth visiting that I'll leave it to you to discover what there is to see in your own district. Many have been excavated, and your local archaeological society will be able to tell you of the nearest sites.

More mysterious are the stone-walled forts to be found in parts of Cornwall, Wales, Ireland and Scotland. There are various types, but those that fascinate me most are the *brochs* or towers, of which the best specimens are found in northern Scotland. They are circular in shape, with walls twelve feet or more thick at the base and standing forty or more feet high. They look rather like the castle towers of a thousand years later. Belonging to the Iron Age, they date from some time between 100 BC and AD 100, and

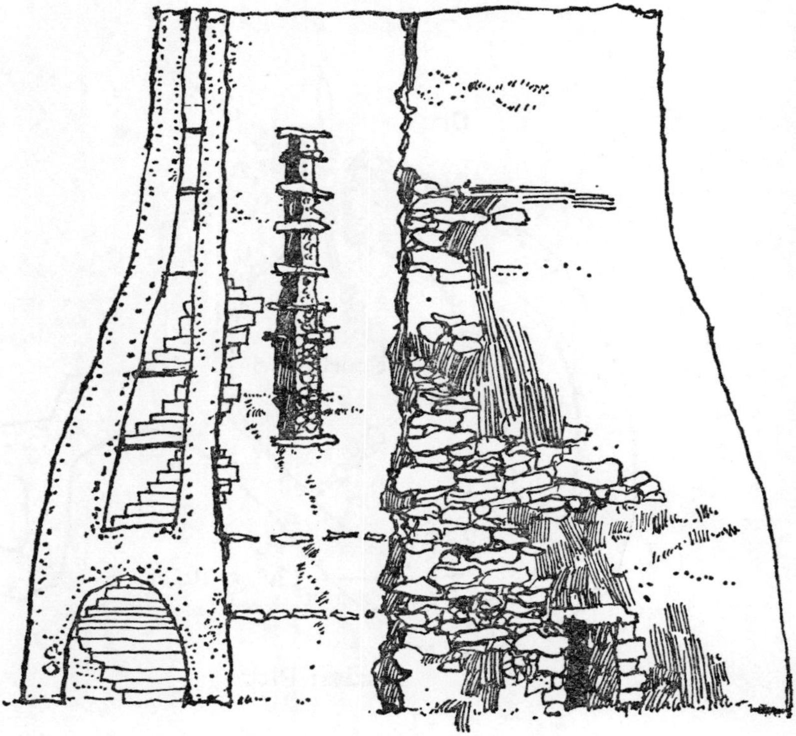

A Scottish broch, showing stairway in walls (based upon Mousa, Shetland Islands)

were the homes of farming communities who migrated by sea from south-west Britain. The Shetland Isles provide some fine specimens, of which the most outstanding is the solitary tower on the island of Mousa.

The remains of houses and settlements of the Iron Age are not easy to track down, except in areas where stone was the principal building material. At Chysauster, near Penzance, a stone-walled village of streets and houses has been preserved. The Isle of Man – another archaeologist's treasure-house, containing monuments from almost every period from the Stone Age to Viking times and later – has several Iron Age

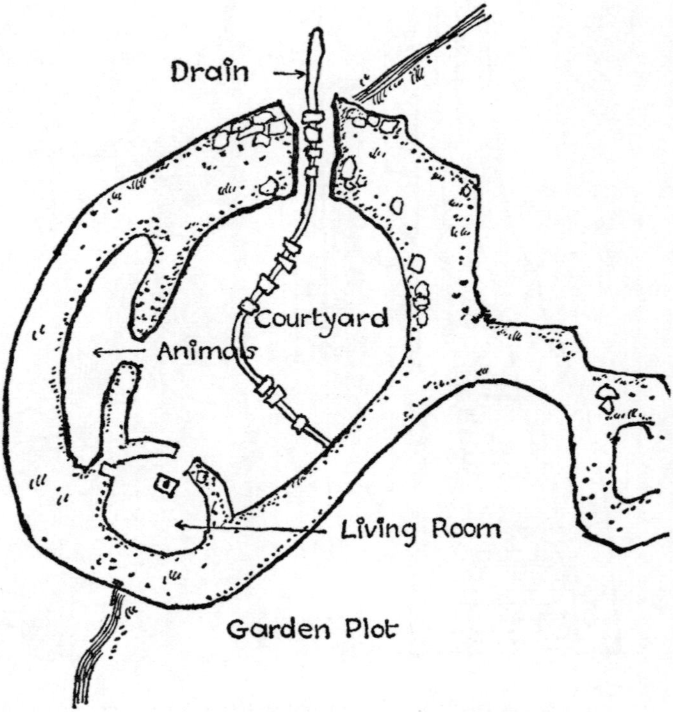

Plan of a 'courtyard house', Chysauster, Cornwall

sites, of which the most interesting is a settlement at Braaid, where the stone walls of two circular houses are to be seen.

The Iron Age was a great time for building earthworks, and there is a need for amateur archaeologists to help solve the problems associated with the constructions of these structures. Often they run for miles across the countryside.* An example is the tremendous ditch called the Devil's Dyke, at Wheathampstead in Hertfordshire. The sign at the entrance states: 'This entrenchment was part of a British city built in the first century BC. It was probably here that Julius Caesar defeated the British king Cassivellaunus in 54 BC.' Cassivellaunus was the British chieftain who ruled the district north of the Thames at the time of Caesar's second invasion, and he is the first actual personage to be named in our history books.

Stanwick earthworks, in the North Riding of Yorkshire, should also be visited; like Maiden Castle far to the south, they impress by the sheer bulk of their defences. The history of the two places seems to have been similar, for the Stanwick earthworks were built to oppose the Roman advance and, like Maiden Castle, failed to stop the irresistible legions.

In search of Roman remains. Something about the phrase 'Roman remains' appeals to most people's imagination. The spell of Rome lingers on in Britain, even after 2,000 years.

To experience that spell, stand perhaps by the North Gate of the ruined fort of Vercovicium on the Roman Wall, in Northumberland, and gaze down over that wonderful panorama of dark woodlands, basalt crags and blue lakes – surely one of the grandest views in all England! There you must feel something of the immense glamour of the past; and in particular of that period of our past shaped by the Romans, who left us the remains of so many forts and towns, roads, villas, baths and theatres.

This is not the place to retell Roman history. Read *Roman Britain* by I. A. Richmond (Penguin), or *The Great Invasion* (Evans) or *Seeing Roman Britain* (Pan),

* Read *Field Archaeology: Some Notes for Beginners*, issued by the Ordnance Survey, which describes in detail things of which I can make only the briefest mention here.

both the latter by Leonard Cottrell; such books will provide the background knowledge you will need. But seeing the sites of the Roman occupation will bring the words of the history books to life.

The most impressive Roman remains are the military ones. Roman forts are to be found in many mountainous areas. The occupation of Britain was based on three big legionary fortresses at York, Chester and Caerleon, in South Wales. The Roman army consisted of the legions, brigades of 5,000–6,000 highly-trained infantry, and the auxiliaries, cohorts of 500–1,000 men, divided into cavalry and infantry. The auxiliaries guarded the frontiers, while the legionaries did the hard fighting. Soldiers also acted as a labour corps, and built roads, forts, walls and buildings whose remains are to be seen today.

Out of the first simple earthworks within which the soldiers pitched their tents arose the more complex stone structures with moats and battlemented walls, two main streets crossing at right angles, and the military headquarters in the centre. These forts were usually rectangular in shape, and varied in size from a few acres to over a hundred. Those of average size held about 500 men. The chief buildings were the commanding officer's house, the granaries to hold a year's supply of grain, the workshops, armouries and bakeries. The rest of the space inside the walls would be occupied by barrack buildings, long narrow structures each of which housed a century, or 80 men. Outside the fort would be a walled enclosure where the soldiers' families lived, together with traders and camp-followers.

Remains of legionary fortresses are scanty, though York retains the bastion known as the Multangular Tower and part of the wall. Chester still has part of its walls, and the south-eastern corner of the fort. Caerleon, headquarters of the Second Legion, still has

Map of Roman Britain (simplified)

some of its wall, and the finest example of a Roman amphitheatre in Britain. Cardiff Castle, Hardknott, in Cumberland and Melandra Castle, in Derbyshire, are typical Roman forts. The four Cawthorn Camps on the moors north of Pickering, Yorkshire, are unique, being built for the training of Roman soldiers.

Grandest of all Roman remains in Britain is Hadrian's Wall, stretching across the country almost from the North Sea to the Solway Firth. This Roman wall was originally nearly 73 miles long, and though parts have been removed to build houses, miles of it still stand. As well as the Wall, there is the great ditch called the Vallum, and the remains of various forts and watch-towers. Near Corbridge is the Roman town of *Corstopitum,* which was the military supply depot for the Wall.

The Wall was completed in AD 128 by the Emperor Hadrian. Its original dimensions are believed to have been an average width of eight feet, a height of sixteen to eighteen feet. The Wall had a core of rubble and an outer facing of stone blocks. At intervals of a few miles were forts, each occupying several acres and garrisoned by 500–1,000 men. Between the large forts were smaller ones called mile-castles; and between these again, at shorter intervals, were watch-towers or turrets. The path running along the top of the Wall was patrolled night and day.

It's important to realize that the Wall wasn't just a fighting-platform, from which Roman soldiers kept invading Caledonians at bay. Its purpose was less to halt invading armies than to check the movements of smugglers or raiders. The Romans did not fight behind walls, but out in the open, relying on their superior armament and organisation. Each fort had a gate opening north through which the legionaries could march out to confront the enemy.

The forts of *Vercovicium* (Housesteads) and *Cilurnum* (Chesters) are among the best-preserved in the country.

At Housesteads the ramparts still stand several yards high. You can see the little arena where the soldiers wrestled, the ruts made by chariot wheels, the room which housed the imperial standards, saluted by every legionary as he passed. Here also is the strange 'Murder Room' where two skeletons were found, one with a dagger in its back.

East and west of Housesteads lie other forts – *Aesica, Vindolanda, Camboglanna*. Then there's Win-

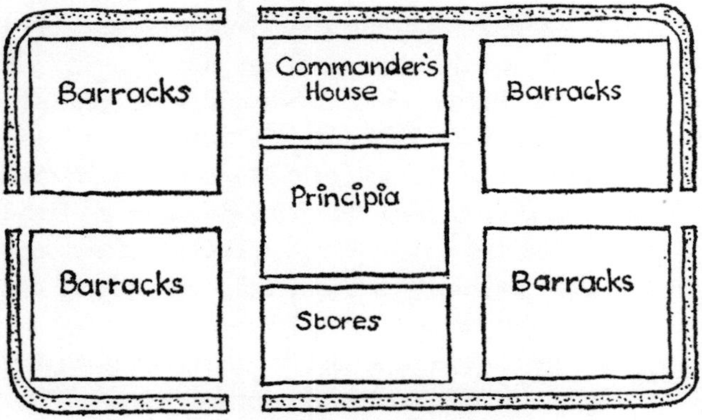

Plan of typical Roman Fort

shields Crag, where the Wall reaches its highest point at 1,250 feet above sea-level, the 'Turf Wall' at Birdoswald, and the quarry near Acomb where 1,800 years ago three Roman quarrymen cut their names – Securus, Maternus and Jestus. By bicycle or afoot, you can spend an exciting week or two discovering all that remains of the Roman Wall between the Solway and the Tyne.*

The most imposing Roman remains in Britain, after Hadrian's Wall, are the 'Forts of the Saxon Shore'. As

* A good preparation for such an expedition is to read Rudyard Kipling's *Puck of Pook's Hill* (now in paperback), which recreates the atmosphere of the days when the Wall was still manned. Ordnance Survey produces a really beautiful map of the Wall that's well worth carrying with you.

the raids by the Anglo-Saxons increased in intensity during the 4th century, the Romans erected a series of great fortresses, extending from Southampton Water to the Wash. These were different from the forts of earlier times, and were equipped with bastions, or big circular towers, from which flanking fire could be directed at attackers. These bastions supported the giant catapults which took the place of artillery in Roman times.

Some of these great forts have been destroyed by coastal erosion, but four have been preserved and are well worth visiting. They are Burgh Castle, near Great Yarmouth, Richborough Castle, near Ramsgate, Pevensey Castle, near Eastbourne, and Portchester Castle near Portsmouth. Though termed 'castles', they mustn't be confused with the castles of the Middle Ages; the two types of fortification are separated in time by nearly a thousand years. Later castles were sometimes built inside Roman forts.

Richborough is one of the most interesting Roman ruins in England, and contains a huge, cross-shaped mass of masonry believed to be the base of the great monument erected by the Emperor Claudius to commemorate his conquest of Britain. Pevensey, the *Castrum Anderida* of the Romans, still stands surrounded by walls ten feet thick and thirty feet high. The fate of this fortress is known; in AD 491, the Saxons took the place by storm and all the inhabitants perished by sword and fire.

At Dover the octagonal tower of a Roman lighthouse stands inside the castle walls, while inside the walls of Scarborough Castle are the remains of a signal station erected by the Romans as part of their defences against attack by Saxon raiders.

Roman forts are to be found in Scotland, but more interesting is the Antonine Wall, an earthern rampart and ditch built about AD 140 to strengthen the line of fortifications laid down by Agricola. It ran from Bo'ness on the Forth to West Kilpatrick on the Clyde, a distance of thirty-seven miles. A line of forts, with small watch-towers between, gave the wall added strength. You can study a section of it near Bonnybridge, with the remains of the fort called Rough Castle.

This wall marked the northern limits of the Roman Empire until the province of Caledonia was abandoned and the wall across northern England became the boundary.

Roman Towns and Houses. The Ordnance Survey map of Roman Britain (which you should consult) shows about seventy towns and over seven hundred villas or settlements. Most of the towns were situated in south-eastern England – Kent, Surrey, Sussex, Hampshire – with populated areas in Dorset and Somerset. The Cotswolds was a thickly-populated area, with other settlements in the Severn Valley and Shropshire. In eastern England the settled areas extended into East Anglia, Lincolnshire and Yorkshire.

A network of Roman roads traversed the country, linking the seaports and London with the towns and settlements inland. Many of these roads lie underneath the motor-roads in use today. It's an interesting exercise in field-archaeology to try and trace the routes of some of these Roman roads. If you want to see what a Roman road looked like there's a fine section on show on Wheeldale Moor, in north-east Yorkshire. Another stretch of road is exposed at Blackstone Edge, near Littleborough, Lancashire.

Most Roman towns were built to a uniform plan, rectangular, with streets at right angles. The *forum* or market-place was in the centre. This was the social centre of the town, where goods were offered for sale, and people met to discuss business and to gossip. On one side stood the *basilica* or town hall, where the law courts were held, and on the other sides were shops, temples, public baths. Side-streets would contain inns, workshops, warehouses and the homes of merchants and officials.

Outside the towns, alongside the roads, were the cemeteries, with tombs of stone or tiles, standing in rows, and the amphitheatre where shows of various kinds were held.

Britain does not contain any complete Roman public buildings, if only because their sites are usually occupied by modern structures. At Caerwent, Monmouthshire, the south wall of the Roman town still stands, and is one of the finest examples of Roman walling left in England. Silchester, near Reading, retains its Roman walls, though the buildings inside them are buried under grass. (Reading Museum contains an excellent collection of objects dug up from the buried city).

Roman town gates can be seen at Lincoln – the Newport Arch – and at Colchester – the Balkerne Gate. The Roman *forum* is preserved at Leicester, and the massive arched wall behind it was part of the *basilica*. The site of the *forum* and *basilica* can be seen at Wroxeter, near Shrewsbury, which was Viroconium – 'The White City in the Woods'. The massive walls of the public baths still tower up to a height of several yards.

Gladiatorial shows were held in most towns, and an almost complete example of a Roman amphitheatre can be seen at Caerleon, Monmouthshire. At St Albans one can see the only Roman theatre discovered in this country.

Public bath houses were a prominent feature of every town. They were social centres where conversation was almost as important as bathing. Bath itself is perhaps the only town where the remains of Roman public buildings can be seen in a good state of preservation. You *must* see these, and the underground spring where hot water gushes out of the earth. Baths can be seen at Wall, in Staffordshire, which was a posting-station. Baths can also often be seen at Roman villas.

What did the persons who used these baths look like? The mummified body of a Romano-Briton dug up in Yorkshire gives us some idea – he wore a green cloak, scarlet tunic, yellow stockings and leather sandals.

Reconstruction of Roman villa excavated near St Albans. (*Reproduced by permission of the Ministry of Public Building and Works*)

At Colchester, in Essex, one can enter the crypt of the only large temple discovered in Britain. It was dedicated to the Emperor Claudius, in whose reign the conquest of Britain was made. Hundreds of years later the Normans used it as a base for their castle. An early Christian chapel was found in the Roman villa at Lullingstone, in Kent, which is one of the best-preserved villas in the country. Perhaps the most remarkable religious site of Romano-British times is the temple at Lydney, in Gloucestershire, which, with its inn and bath-house, stands inside an Iron Age fort. In London, a temple of the god Mithras has been preserved.

What about the houses the people lived in? In various parts of the country are the remains of Roman villas. These were not only private houses, the homes of Romano-British families, but were also the headquarters of big agricultural estates. About a thousand villas have been discovered, but there must be many more. Locating the sites of these villas is another job for the amateur archaeologist, and it can be exciting.

The Cotswolds, Oxfordshire, the Isle of Wight, all have numerous villas, and they extend west into Dorset and northwards into Lincolnshire and Yorkshire.

These villas were the homes of British aristocrats who had adopted the Roman style of living. Villas varied in size, from small, simple farmhouses to stately mansions. Such houses were built of wood on a stone or brick foundation, and consisted of a series of rooms opening off a courtyard or corridor. They had mosaic floors, walls of painted plaster, a suite of baths, glass windows. Some had twenty or thirty rooms.

Such a villa can be visited at Chedworth, in Gloucestershire. It was discovered in 1864 when a man digging a ferret out of a rabbit hole revealed part of a mosaic floor, made up of thousands of pieces of coloured stone and brick. Later excavation exposed to view the rooms, courtyards and corridors of a great Roman mansion. Now the villa is cared for by the National Trust, and the visitor can walk from room to room and get a clear idea of the lay-out of a wealthy Romano-British landowner's home. Also visible are a blacksmith's shop, a laundry and a bakery.

Other Roman villas can be visited – there's one at Brading, on the Isle of Wight, and others at Newport, on the same island: at Bignor, in Sussex: at Folkestone and at Northleigh, in Oxfordshire. I have already mentioned the one at Lullingstone, in Kent, which is perhaps the most impressive of them all.

From the Romans to 1066. There aren't a lot of remains dating from the period between the end of Roman

Britain and the Battle of Hastings in 1066. From the day of the Anglo-Saxons, the Danes and the Norsemen, what does one find? Some earthworks, a few churches, some camps and settlement-sites: the sites also of perhaps a dozen Celtic monasteries. Western Britain remained Celtic, with its own special and intriguing

Greensted, Essex. The only Saxon timber church left in England

monuments – churches and inscribed stones, forts and round towers.

Our Anglo-Saxon ancestors built mainly in wood, so most of their halls and houses vanished long ago; but at Greensted-Juxta-Ongar,* in Essex, a unique wooden church has somehow survived, with the walls of the nave made of split oak trunks. The church at Escomb, in Durham, shows that the Saxons could build in stone; and at Bradford-on-Avon, in Wiltshire, is the finest complete Saxon church in this country.

* This name itself is a piece of, as it were, verbal archaeology – 'juxta' being the Latin for 'next to'.

Another fine Saxon church exists at Brixworth, in Northamptonshire, and there are Saxon chapels in a number of places – such as the one at Bradwell Waterside, in Essex, built with materials from the Roman fort.

I once made a special journey to visit St Martin's Church, Canterbury, said to be the oldest church still in use in England. It is believed to be nearly 1,500 years old, its Saxon builders having used stones from Roman buildings.

But the most impressive monument of Anglo-Saxon times is the great earthwork known as Offa's Dyke, which stretches across the country from the River Dee to the River Wye, a distance of over 130 miles. It recalls the name of Offa, the king of Mercia (the 'Middle Kingdom') in the 8th century. He conquered much of this territory from the Welsh, and the dyke was constructed to mark the boundary. Though the dyke has been destroyed in places, a well-preserved section of the great earthwork can be seen north-west of the town of Knighton, in Radnorshire.

It is difficult to associate the Norsemen and the Danes – the Vikings of films and novels – with the placid British countryside, but they sailed their long-ships to Britain and their descendants lived here for centuries – and are still here! York, Lincoln, Nottingham, Derby, Leicester and Stamford were Scandinavian strongholds. Dublin was capital of a Viking kingdom. Danish colonists occupied much of eastern England. Norsemen lived in Scotland, the Lake District, parts of Lancashire and Cheshire, south Wales and the Isle of Man. The Shetland and Orkney Islands remained Norwegian much later than the rest of the British Isles.

Remains of Norse and Danish settlements are rare in England and Scotland, though some houses have been uncovered on Malham Moor, in Yorkshire. There must be other sites, if only somebody would look for them. At Jarlshof, in Shetland, is the most complete Norse settlement discovered in Britain. There one can see what is left of a group of houses of an actual Viking settlement. It is one of the most remarkable archaeological sites ever excavated in the British Isles, and well worth making a long journey to see. Near the ruined Viking settlement rises a *broch,* or round tower, built by earlier Iron Age settlers. The remains of a Bronze Age settlement can also be explored, as well as the ruins of a medieval farmstead and later buildings. All this – three thousand years of history – on a windswept promontory jutting out into the sea.

Another settlement of Norse 'long houses' has been uncovered at Birsay, Orkney, together with an early Christian settlement. The Orkney Islands contain many fascinating archaeological sites – prehistoric, Norse, medieval – and an interesting and exciting holiday could be spent travelling by boat among the different islands, investigating them.

The same might be said of the Isle of Man, which was also a Norse kingdom for centuries; it is easily accessible from Liverpool. At Braaid are the remains of a boat-shaped house of a type known in Denmark during the Viking Age, while adjoining it is a huge rectangular house, now in ruins, of Norse type. And a few yards away are the remains of a big circular Celtic house of the Iron Age people who were living on Man when the Scandinavian settlers arrived.

Foundations of another house of Norse type can be seen at Cronk ny Merriu, on the coast south of Douglas. A full-scale reconstruction of the walls gives some idea of the original appearance of such a building.

Also on the island are the ruins of many *keeills,* which were early Christian chapels. At Maughold are the

Viking relics – Axe heads and swords

ruins of three of these, with a number of decorated and inscribed stones of the Norse period.

On St Patrick's Isle, off the ancient harbour of Peel, is a Round Tower of the type built to provide refuge

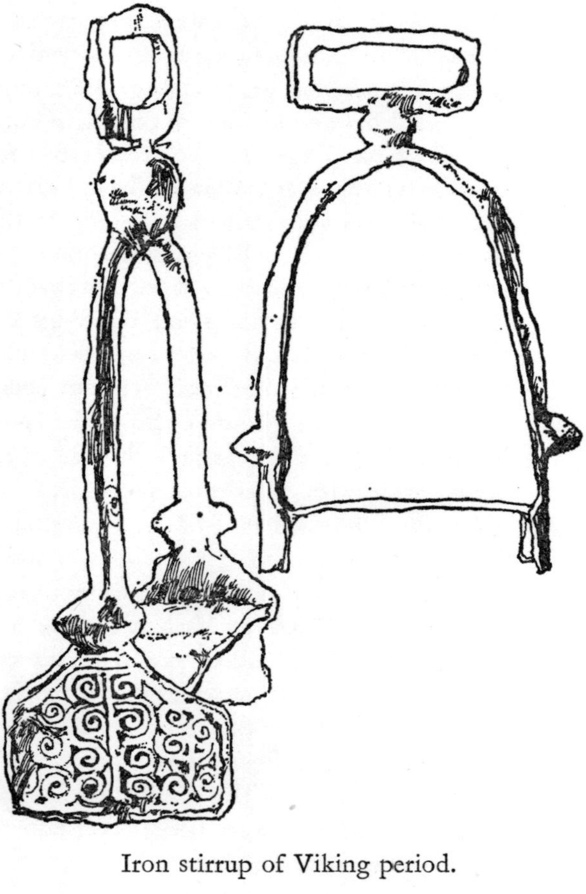

Iron stirrup of Viking period.

from Viking raiders. And inside the stone walls that run round this island are a castle and a cathedral.

Castle Rushen, on the opposite side of Man, is one of the most complete castles in Britain, its high, four-towered keep preserving the masonry of the original stronghold which was the seat of government of the later Norse kings.

At Cregneash, near the ancient Mull stone circle, is the Manx Open Air Folk Museum. Cregneash is a survival of an old Celtic type of farming settlement (a *clachan* as it would be called in western Scotland), whose inhabitants between them worked 300 acres of scattered corn-plots and rough grazing. Since an open air museum is one formed of complete buildings and groups of buildings, with their everyday furnishings, various buildings at Cregneash have been saved from destruction so that visitors can see something of the old-time Manx way of living. One building is a smithy, another a turner's shop, a third a weaver's house. A little group of thatched stone buildings comprises a croft or farmstead, with thirty acres of arable fields and grazing; some of it lies open, without enclosing field walls. The weaver's house contains the last handloom in the district, and the turner's shop still has a joiner's treadle-lathe with other tools and gear.

Of two other sites from this period that have impressed me enormously, one was in Ireland: Glendalough, 'The City of the Seven Churches', situated in a valley in the Wicklow Mountains, south of Dublin. A monastery was founded here in the 6th century and became one of the most renowned centres of learning in Europe. Some of the ruined buildings date from this time, though many have been rebuilt during succeeding centuries. The city was finally destroyed by fire in the 14th century and left deserted.

The other great site is that of Tintagel Castle, on the rocky coast of North Cornwall. I wasn't drawn there by the ruined castle itself, mistakenly held to be the home of King Arthur, but by the remains of the Celtic monastic establishment that is preserved on the headland, above the leaping waves. The ruins of Celtic monasteries are known in Wales and Ireland, but this is the only one to have been excavated in England. These early Christian monasteries are separated by a gap of many centuries from the monasteries of later times, the ruins of which are to be found in many parts of the British Isles. They date from the period known as the Dark Ages when Roman

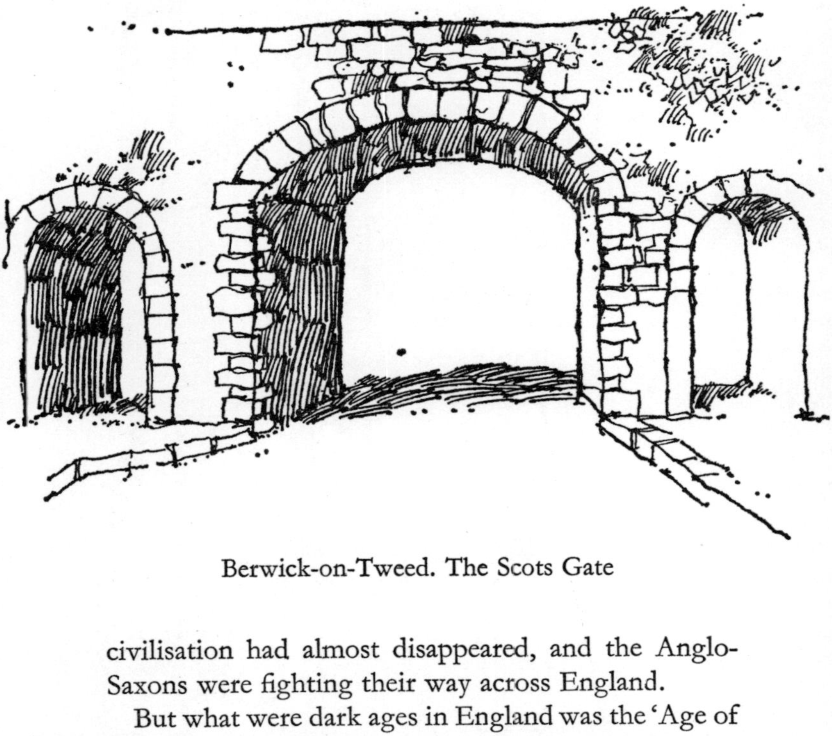

Berwick-on-Tweed. The Scots Gate

civilisation had almost disappeared, and the Anglo-Saxons were fighting their way across England.

But what were dark ages in England was the 'Age of Saints' in Cornwall, Wales, Scotland and Ireland. Many early monasteries were founded by missionaries who travelled from country to country in skin-covered boats. Often these monasteries were built on islands – Caldey and Bardsey Islands off the coast of Wales, Holy Island off Northumberland, the Isles of Scilly. Most spectacular of all is the well-preserved monastery of Skellig Michael, whose stone-walled buildings crown the summit of a steep rock miles out in the Atlantic off the coast of Kerry. To reach this place is an adventure in itself.

This brief survey of the outstanding sites of the period will, I hope, have given you some feeling for

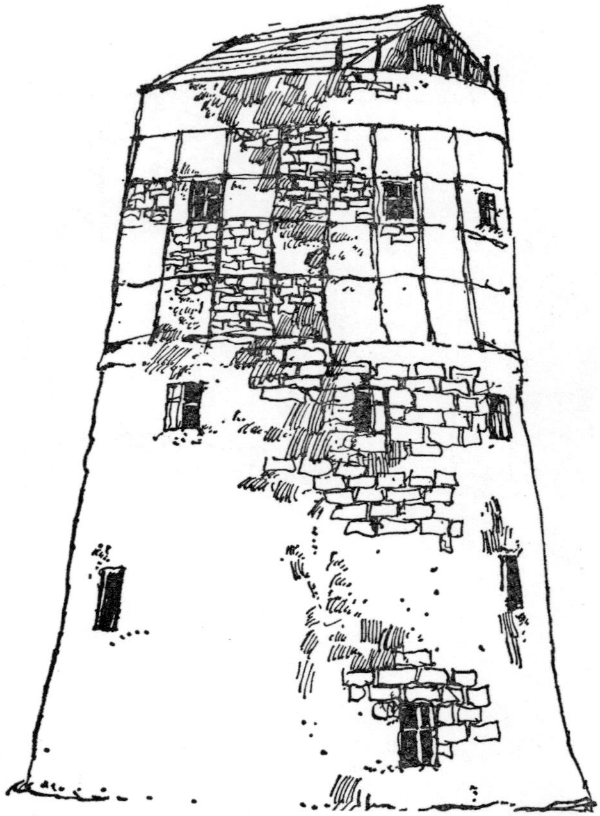

Great Yarmouth. The South-West Tower of the Town Walls

what there is to see. All those I have mentioned stand out in my own memory. There are hundreds more – many, probably, not too far from your own home.

I have said very little about castles, monasteries, churches, cathedrals, famous houses. To refer even to the outstanding castles would fill this book. All these structures are well documented, and your local library will give the references. My own choice of castles that a beginner should see would certainly include a wonderful group along the coast of Northumberland – Bamburgh, Dunstanburgh, Warkworth and Alnwick. They are all magnificent. North Wales yields another fine crop – Conway, Caernarvon, Beaumaris and Harlech. Among my own favourites are Carisbrooke, in the Isle of Wight, and Cardiff Castle, which has a reconstructed Roman gateway. But this is really a matter of personal choice and exploration.

I'll end this survey of that part of our past that ended in 1066 with a suggestion. Why not visit the walled towns of Britain? There are more than many people imagine. York is the finest, but Chester runs it a close second. The gates and towers of both cities are a sight worth seeing. Then there are Berwick-upon-Tweed and Londonderry, in Northern Ireland, both of which had their walls guarded by cannon; and the walls and towers of Conway and Caernarvon in north Wales, which stand beside the sea, as do the walls of Tenby and Chepstow in the south. Newcastle-on-Tyne retains more of its medieval fortifications than is generally realised. Great Yarmouth, Colchester, Southampton, Exeter – all these towns and cities have considerable lengths of their old town walls standing. And town gates can still be seen at Sandwich, in Kent, Ludlow, in Shropshire, Alnwick, in Northumberland, and Beverley in Yorkshire.

I shall deal with the archaeological remains of later centuries in the chapter on industrial archaeology. Meanwhile, this seems the moment to discuss the activity that most people associate with archaeology: that of digging.

Let's Go Digging

With such a title for this chapter, it will seem odd if I begin with a warning: DON'T DIG!

All amateur archaeologists experience the urge to grab a pick or spade and hack their way into some exciting-looking earthwork or ruin, in the hope of making a find.

DON'T!

Later on, perhaps, but not now.

The fact is that archaeological investigation today is a highly-skilled and scientific activity. The days of hacking and rough digging are over. Much of the evidence by means of which the history of a site can be reconstructed is contained in the stratified layers of material hidden below the ground surface. This evidence is often so minute and so fragile that the over-hasty beginner is likely to overlook it or, worse still, to destroy it without realising that he is doing so. Once that evidence is destroyed, the chance of a more experienced person being able to make use of it is lost for ever.

So DON'T DIG: not, at any rate, to satisfy your own curiosity. That was the fault of the old-time antiquarians, who hacked their way into burial-mounds and Roman villas, destroying vital evidence. They were little better than ruthless treasure-hunters. Little of real value was learned by such clumsy methods. Interpreting and recording information about a site is the aim of modern digging, not just searching for valuables.

So resist the urge to dig until you have acquired the training and the experience, under skilled supervision. Remains from the past which have waited two or three thousand years can wait a few years more until you have gained the necessary technical competence.

If you *must* dig, confine your activities to something simple, such as cutting trial trenches to help identify an old road. This will teach you something about field-archaeology. But even here it's best first to learn to know what you are looking for. Helping to uncover a disused railway-line is an archaeological exercise which will give you some healthy exercise and experience, without risk of harm to the evidence.

Why then did I give this chapter the title 'Let's Go Digging'? Because there are plenty of opportunities nowadays to learn to do the job the *right* way. If you want to gain experience and technical knowledge you can get it by taking part in one of the dozens of 'digs' which take place in all parts of the British Isles each year. These 'digs' deal with every type of archaeological excavation, from the investigation of prehistoric burials and settlement-sites, to the uncovering of Roman, Saxon, medieval and industrial archaeological sites – glass-works, kilns, old furnaces and factories.

Many of these excavations are organized by universities and others by local societies. The Ministry of Works is probably the biggest organizer of such 'digs' – nearly a hundred in a recent year. The Ministry's 1969–70 budget for archaeological projects, for example, was £170,000, of which £150,000 was spent on sites in England, £4,600 in Scotland, and £15,000 in Wales. Generally it is only on digs organized or supported by the Ministry of Public Building and Works that volunteers are paid – £1 a day subsistence pay, and £2 travel allowance. The digging season lasts from Easter to October.

Every summer sees hundreds of amateur archaeologists heading for sites where a Ministry excavation is in progress. Students, nurses, housewives, typists, teachers, shop assistants – whatever their way of earning a living, all are prepared to spend their holidays helping to excavate a prehistoric burial ground, a Roman villa, a Saxon town – anything. They live in camps organized by the Ministry, work during the day under the supervision of the Ministry's supervisors, play darts or skittles at night, or just talk.

The Council for British Archaeology, which is the co-ordinating body for over 250 local archaeological societies, twenty or so universities, and over eighty museums, produces a monthly calendar of excavations, which gives details of the places where volunteers are needed. This Calendar goes out to over 2,000 subscribers in the British Isles, America, Europe and parts of Africa.

The address is: Council for British Archaeology, 8 St Andrew's Place, London, N.W.1. The subscription to the Calendar of Excavations is 10s., post free. Published from March to September, it gives details of the times and sites of the different 'digs' and the names of the directors in charge. Applicants must write to the director concerned, enclosing a stamped addressed envelope for his reply. Over 2,500 inquiries a year are made by people who want to gain practical experience.

As I've said, there is a great difference between the modern archaeologist working on scientific lines, with definite problems to solve and definite techniques for answering them, and the old-time antiquary. With a few honourable exceptions, the old-timer was more of a curio-hunter than a scientist, and was more concerned with what he would find in a tomb or building than in the structure itself. His attitude was that of a collector, eager for trophies – coins, pottery, weapons, jewellery and so forth – and, in his desire to discover as quickly as possible whether these were forthcoming, he paid little attention to the relationship between a find and its surroundings.

This attitude was little better than that of the plain treasure-hunter, who hacked his way into mounds and buildings, intent only on finding something valuable, and thus destroyed for ever any evidence which might have helped in identifying or dating the site. In either case, no records were kept, and the sum-total of facts added to our accumulated knowledge of the past was practically nothing.

Modern archaeological excavation has certain well-defined aims as well as its specialized technique. Its primary aim is less to find things than to gain a complete record of the various phases which a site has undergone. A haphazard collection of objects about which no precise facts are known is of little value. A full description of a find, together with details of the position in which it was discovered, plus a plan and a photograph, is of more value than the possession of an actual object about which we have no details. It is just as important to know the surroundings in which an object was found as to possess the object itself. This changed attitude has resulted in more being found out about the archaeology of Britain in the last fifty years than had been discovered previously in a century.

The evidence upon which modern archaeology depends for its reconstruction of a site is often of such a minute and fragmentary nature that it is not easily perceived by the untrained eye. A site which has been long inhabited retains evidence of each past stage of its history in layers of matter of varying colour and texture, and it is by the aid of the bits of bone, pottery, and other materials found in these layers that the dates of the various stages of history can very often be determined. These 'habitation' or 'occupation' layers were usually disregarded by earlier archaeologists, who thought only in terms of coins or other recognisable data, and who did not realize the value of the other remains upon which they came.

This is why the impulse to dig down as soon as possible and discover what lies underneath is fatal, because it means the destruction of the stratified layers upon which the archaeologist relies for his record of the site. A change in the colour or texture of the soil, a few rust-coloured stains indicative of vanished metal or bone, minute fragments of wood or fibre – all this evidence for dating may be quickly ruined by the overhasty worker.

Consider the problem which confronts the archaeologist. Here, let us say, eighteen hundred years ago, was a Romano-British house. But what sort of a house – palatial villa, small country residence, or rough farmhouse – we do not know. This building probably stood for a couple of centuries, perhaps more. Successive generations of our ancestors lived within its walls, altered its internal arrangements, left various relics of their occupation. In the end, perhaps, the house was abandoned and allowed to fall into ruins, or destroyed by fire, as many Romano-British houses were. Maybe, centuries later, the stonework of the walls was carted away to build other structures, or perhaps the ruin was gradually buried out of sight by the accumulation of soil. Possibly trees grew up on the site, their roots wrenching apart the hidden foundations, or a stream changed its course and flowed over part of the vanished building.

Now the archaeologist has to reconstruct the history of that almost-destroyed dwelling by excavating and piecing together the bits of evidence he finds there. He knows that buried out of sight are the remains of those successive generations who inhabited the house – bits of pottery they discarded, implements they used, coins which dropped into cracks and corners, other material reminders of their daily lives – all these things arranged in layers which can be dated, provided they are uncovered without too much disturbance.

Perhaps there will be the charred timbers and tiles of the roof, together with the bones of wild and domestic animals mingled with the remains of the humans who met their deaths there. Into that accumulated mass the archaeologist must dig, trying to build up from the relics of masonry, metal-work, pottery, and other oddments some details of the life-story of the people who lived in that house eighteen centuries before. That, using this evidence, he can provide us with so much detail of life in Britain so long ago, is a tribute to the archaeological techniques that have been developed during the past few decades.

Britain, we have to remember, isn't Egypt or Italy, where it may be possible to find masses of archaeological material in a more or less undisturbed state of preservation. Ours is a small island, much worked over and lived in, and has been subject to both an agricultural and an industrial revolution; so that we often have to grub about long and hard for such scanty remains from the past as are to be found.

Archaeologists excavating a site have three main aims. One is to excavate the site so as to expose the successive occupation-levels in turn; the second aim is to record and preserve anything of *archaeological* value found in each layer; the third is to make a plan and take photographs of each stage of the work as it proceeds. A 'dig' usually owes its beginning to some reference in literature, or perhaps to the chance discovery of masonry, or to other finds which indicate that a site is worth investigating. A series of trial-trenches is then dug across the site in the hope of uncovering sufficient remains to give a clue to the identity of the place. The area between the trenches may then be opened up to reveal the complete outline of the structure.

The trenches are excavated spadeful by spadeful, and, if time permits, the displaced material is passed through a sieve before being removed to the waste-dumps. Owing to the high cost of excavation nowadays, and to lack of time and shortage of skilled supervisors, this high standard is not always possible, and often it is left to individual workers to keep a close watch on the soil they are discarding. For finer work, such as cleaning masonry and smoothing occupation-levels, a trowel is used, while all surfaces have to be cleaned with a brush before photographing.

When a layer indicating an occupation is reached it is smoothed with a trowel. Its depth from the surface, and the exact position of any coins, sherds, or other objects, are measured and recorded. Containers are placed by each trench, into which finds are put. Each container has a label bearing the date, description of the area being worked, and the alphabetical designation of the trench: for example, Area 2, Trench B. A separate container is used for each level so that finds from different layers do not get mixed together.

Great care has to be taken to see that objects from exposed upper layers do not fall to the bottom of the trench and become mixed with objects found at the lower level, as this may invalidate the dating of both levels. If this should happen, and the person in charge of the dig is a purist in such matters, he will have no option but to discard all the evidence, and start afresh.

What the archaeologist hopes to get is a 'closed group' of finds: that is, occupation-layers which have been sealed off by later accumulations of soil, and have thus not been disturbed by later intrusions, so there is no question of interference with the material used for dating. When a site has been interfered with by the digging of post-holes, rubbish-pits, or other excavations, remains of a later date may intrude to a lower level, and thus lead to confusion in dating.

All finds need cleaning and numbering before the job of identifying them can begin. Pottery needs scrubbing with a brush to remove all mud. In addition to the details already mentioned, a number must be given to each object, so that it can be referred to again when wanted. This number can be inked on a piece of pottery, but for other finds a small card containing these particulars is attached. Later, somebody will have the job of making a card-index of all finds, on which the various details of their history are recorded.

Where literary references and coinage are not available, pottery is much used as a means of dating a site. Pottery is often of such a comparatively bulky and fragile nature, which would render it unsuitable for lengthy transportation, that it may safely be assumed to belong to certain localised areas. Also, changing fashions in shapes, rims, and handles make it easier to attribute pots to certain periods, and so give a time-sequence to which different phases of a culture can be assigned.

When a fragment of pottery is found, the chances are that other pieces will be found nearby, and it may be possible to fit them together and get a complete pot. Commonly one does not get a whole pot, but may find a series of rims or handles which are useful for dating. Sometimes objects of wood or metal have so disintegrated that only a 'ghost' or discoloured outline in the soil is left. Yet that shadow may once have been a piece of timber, or an object of metal or bone, and it may still be possible to get some idea of what it was if one works round it carefully with a trowel.

One has to watch, also, for such things as post-holes, which may contain decayed timber; stonework changed by the action of heat or water; and the varying nature of the subsoil in which one is working.

The interpretation of the evidence is in the province of the expert rather than that of the ordinary field-worker. Coins, bones, pieces of pottery, and metal can all be handed over to someone who has a specialised knowledge of such objects, and the information they supply can be incorporated in the final report on the site. There is usually little time and opportunity during a dig to make more than a superficial examination of the finds, and they must wait until later for a thorough study of their significance. Only then can all the evidence be correlated and a detailed history of the site be worked out.

In excavation and in field-archaeology a knowledge of subjects associated with archaeology will come in useful. Even an elementary knowledge of geology, anthropology, architecture, agriculture and engineering may help. To know something of building construction, of industrial processes such as the making of pottery, textiles and metal implements, of farming methods and animal husbandry, can play a part in the solution of problems. It is startling sometimes to observe how objects in everyday use – tools, designs, instruments – have hardly changed in essentials for two thousand years. You should learn something of fashions in clothing, tastes in food, amusements, religious symbolism and funeral ceremonial; there is hardly a branch of human knowledge that may not at some time be of use to the archaeologist, for his subject deals with every aspect of how people have lived and worked in the past.

Museums are a great help in this matter of interpretation of finds, for they help us to visualize bones and stones in their original setting. Never lose sight of the fact that the aim of archaeology is not just to uncover 'finds', but to deduce the way of life of the people who used them. One can learn something about the Old Stone Age, for example, by studying the stone tools in daily use by the aborigines of Central Australia today. Archaeological material should be studied in conjunction with ethnological collections*, since this brings out most forcibly the extent to which the archaeologist is handicapped by the perishability of his materials. For

* Ethnology is the scientific study of human races, of their cultures and customs.

instance, the richness of the material culture of the Australian aborigines is chiefly in wood and other perishable materials, which would not survive to be dug up by the archaeologist, yet their stone implements which would survive are not very impressive, nor would they give any reliable impression of the life of the people who made them.

It will be seen from all this that the days of haphazard, happy-go-lucky digging are past. Technical knowledge is necessary if an excavation is to serve some useful purpose. So do not treat a 'dig' as a sort of outing or picnic, an occasion for larking about, or an opportunity for digging up quantities of fascinating buried objects. You might dig for days and find very little – perhaps just a crumbling coin or two, or a few fragments of pot. But those few finds, carefully assigned to their particular layers, may prove more instructive than any amount of miscellaneous material.

If, as a beginner, you take part in a large-scale excavation, you will be learning at once any number of useful skills and some basic archaeological facts. Apart from what you learn about stratification and the dating of objects, you will also learn about the different kinds of soil, and the effect of these different soils – gravel, sand, clay and so on – upon structures, bones and other objects that may have been buried in them for centuries. You will learn something, too, about the appearance of structures that have been in ruins, or have been buried, for a long time; what happens to bone, wood, metal, textiles after one century, or a score of centuries, under the ground. If you merely spend a week washing pottery, you will have made a start on one of the most important studies that add up to make the total knowledge and experience of the archaeologist. You may have a chance, also, to learn something of other essential skills: among them, photography, measuring, drawing and surveying.

Archaeology Without a Spade

Working on a big 'dig' in company with a crowd of cheerful, helpful young people is an exhilarating experience. As I have pointed out, the amateur who is keen can learn much. But large-scale excavation is a special form of archaeology, which usually takes place during only part of the year. There is another kind of archaeological investigation that goes on all the time – field archaeology, in which only one or two or maybe half a dozen persons is involved.

You may have seen a group of field-archaeologists at work, striding across fields or moorlands. They will be carrying maps and measuring-tapes, steel probes and compasses. If asked, they might tell you they were tracing the route of a Roman road, or looking for the site of a signal station, or a vanished industrial plant. If you are keen you will feel the urge to do something like this yourself, for though a big 'dig' is fun, the individual digger is only a small cog in a big machine. Field archaeology offers more scope for individual enterprise. You are your own boss, and the success or failure of the enterprise depends on *you*.

If you have ever looked at an Ordnance Survey map and observed the symbols denoting an archaeological site – prehistoric, Roman, medieval or later – you may have wondered why that symbol was put where it was, and who was responsible for its being there. Many of the symbols on the map are the result of field-work undertaken by a large group of hard-working, unpaid, anonymous workers located all over the country. These 'local observers' conduct their investigations in their spare time, sending reports of their finds to the headquarters of the Ordnance Survey, which in due course sees that they are incorporated in new editions of maps.

Thanks to the Ordnance Survey, we in Britain have some of the finest maps in the world, and the field-archaeologist can have the satisfaction of knowing that he has helped, if even in a small way, to produce these.

What is field-archaeology? The obvious reply is that it is archaeological work conducted out-of-doors. But excavation is also carried on out-of-doors, so we must distinguish between two types of archaeological *techniques* – the excavation of sites (frequently on a large scale), and the study of antiquities in the field *without excavation*. A review in *The Listener* of O. G. S. Crawford's book *Archaeology in the Field* (which you must read sometime), gave a definition of field-archaeology which can hardly be improved upon:

'The technique of field archaeology . . . is apparently that archaeological method which requires least expert training; it seems at first sight to demand no more than a knowledge of maps and air photographs, a pair of good boots, and a stout heart.

'In an age when archaeological techniques become increasingly complicated and scientific, when excavation cannot be undertaken except with expert training, field archaeology remains not only a necessity for the professional archaeologist but a delight to those countless amateurs who love being out in the country and observing the non-functional aspects of the cultural landscape around them – from Neolithic long barrows and Bronze Age temples to nineteenth-century disused tramlines and overgrown twentieth-century ox-bow roads'. The writer of these words deserves our applause.

This makes admirable reading, but how do we begin?

Let us suppose that you (or two or three of you) want to go in for field archaeology. You may have got hold of a book produced by the Ordnance Survey called *Field Archaeology: Some Notes for Beginners*. Now, this is an exceedingly useful production, and may be read with much pleasure and profit – later. But it must be admitted that at first sight its 170 pages of detailed analyses of sites can be a bit overwhelming. Let's start with something a little simpler. We can go back to the Ordnance book later.

First we need to know the answers to three questions.

1. What sorts of archaeological jobs are there that I (or we) can do?
2. How do we set about doing them? Or, to put it another way: What knowledge do we need to recognise sites?
3. What equipment do we need?

The answers to the first and last questions will be given later. Let's begin with the second question. What background knowledge does the amateur archaeologist require in order to be able to recognise sites in the field?

The fact is that, apart from the thousands of known sites and monuments in all parts of the British Isles – many of them in the care of the National Trust, the Ministry of Works and private owners – there must remain many others as yet undiscovered. They are undiscovered because nobody with the necessary skill has looked at them in the right way. How are such sites discovered?

This involves another question: How do archaeological sites come to be where they are?

The short answer is that we can expect to find certain types of ancient monument in one kind of country, but not in another. We may expect to find the remains of such structures as Roman villas or medieval houses in districts that have been settled and cultivated for a long time, but not on high, uninhabited moorlands. Conversely, we may expect to find on stony, uncultivated heights such things as prehistoric burial grounds and hut-sites, but *not* Roman villas or medieval villages. Why?

The basic fact of British geography is its division into two types of country – the highland zone and the lowland zone. The lowland zone includes most of south-eastern England. The highland zone consists of most of the uplands of Wales, northern England, and Scotland. The boundary between the two zones runs roughly from the River Tees to Dartmoor. The North Yorkshire moors are a detached area of the highland zone. Between the Welsh mountains and the Pennine heights is the lowland country of Cheshire and Lancashire.

The two zones represent two different types of geology and scenery. The lowland zone is an area of recent, softer rocks – chalks, gravels, sandstones, soft limestones – which produce soils easy to cultivate. The highland zone is a region of ancient, hard rocks – granites, basalts, hard sandstones – where cultivation is difficult, if not impossible. It is a landscape of bleak, inhospitable mountains and moorlands, with a wetter climate.

The lowland zone was the part of Britain first occupied by immigrants from the continent. Occupation of the lowland zone was relatively easy, but occupation of the highland zone was much more difficult.

There is thus a close relationship between geography and human settlement.

The culture of each successive wave of immigrants from the south tended, in the lowland zone, to be replaced by the next wave. Bronze Age was replaced by Iron Age, which was replaced by Roman, which was replaced by Saxon, which was replaced by Norman. This is an over-simplification of a very complex process, but it illustrates the next point I want to make.

In the highland zone it was harder for a new culture to impose itself on an existing culture, and so a fusion of the two took place.

Remnants of older peoples lingered on in mountain areas, while newer peoples occupied the plains. Bronze Age people may have continued living their way of life in the Pennines or the North Yorkshire Moors, while the people of the lowlands were adopting Roman customs and amenities.

These facts of geography act as a rough guide to the types of monument which will be found in different areas. The Roman divided Britain into two zones – a civil zone and a military zone. The Roman military zone corresponded more or less with the geographical highland zone, and their civil zone with the lowland zone. Thus, when seeking Roman remains we may expect to find the remains of forts in the highland zone (but few villas), and the remains of villas and towns in the lowland zone.

With prehistoric remains the reverse applies – new prehistoric sites are less likely to be found by field-archaeologists in the cultivated lowland zone than on the uncultivated moors and mountains of the highland zone.

One exception to the rule that invasion usually took place from the south into the lowland zone was the colonization of parts of the highland zone from the north, from Norway. Therefore we must expect to find Norse settlement-sites in Scotland and its islands, as well as in north-west England, the Isle of Man and Ireland.

Equipped with this knowledge, we are now in a position to advance our studies a stage further. Before you can undertake field-work in your own area, you must know what has already been accomplished. To help you the Ordnance Survey has produced a splendid series of archaeological and historical maps. Most people know of the Ordnance Survey topographical maps which help us to find our way from one place to another. But did you know that the Survey has also produced a number of maps illustrating what is known about various periods of British history? These maps show the field-archaeologist the state of knowledge of any particular historical period, up to the time of publication.

These maps should be consulted, so that you will know what sites have been discovered in your own locality.

1. *Ancient Britain.* This is published in two sheets, at a scale of about 10 miles to one inch, and shows nearly a thousand of the more important and visible antiquities from the earliest times to AD 1066.

2. *Southern Britain in the Iron Age.* This shows the antiquities of this period, at a scale of about ten miles to one inch, in Britain south of a line from Scarborough to the Isle of Man, during the half-millenium before the Roman conquest.

3. *Roman Britain.* This shows on a single sheet, at about sixteen miles to one inch, Britain as it was during the period of Roman occupation from AD 43 to AD 410.

4. *Britain in the Dark Ages.* This shows, at a scale of about 16 miles to one inch, Britain as it was from the end of Roman rule to the time of King Alfred (approximately from AD 410 to AD 870).

5. *Hadrian's Wall.* This shows the whole extent of the Wall on a modern two inches to one mile base map.

6. *Monastic Britain.* This shows the remains of the various monastic establishments and their associated structures from the Norman Conquest to the dissolution of the monasteries in 1539.

Each map is accompanied by a booklet giving additional maps and information relating to the period of history dealt with.

If you consult one or more of these maps (good libraries have them or can obtain them), you will know what there is to see in your neighbourhood, and what gaps in local knowledge remain to be filled in.

These maps are good examples of what are termed *distributional maps*. A distribution map differs from a topographical map in the way in which it shows all the sites and finds associated with a particular culture – whether it be Iron Age, Roman, or so on. Such a map helps one to interpret the extent and development of a culture, so far as our knowledge of it exists at the time of publication. A blank area on such a map may indicate a district devoid of settlement, or it may indicate lack of archaeological investigation. If the latter should be the case, then further discoveries may alter the pattern of distribution of sites on the map. Thus a body of new knowledge is built up.

The use of distribution maps is a common practice in archaeological studies nowadays. It seems logical to us now that knowledge regarding the character and extent of any phase of a country's history can be gained by plotting on a map all the known sites and finds. Credit for the development of this technique must go to the late Dr O. G. S. Crawford, who was the pioneer in this distributional method of archaeological study. He was Archaeology Officer of the Ordnance Survey from 1920 to 1945.

As the pattern of sites on a map is changed by new discoveries, the need for a new edition is indicated. This new map then forms the basis of knowledge about the Bronze Age, Roman period, Dark Ages or Monastic Britain, until it in turn is superseded. That distribution maps have to be re-drawn from time to time is due to the activities of field-workers, who make new discoveries. Many of these workers are young people.

All over the country there are archaeological sites which need investigating. The existence of many of them is unknown and unsuspected. They are hidden underground, below cornfields and pastures, or overgrown by woodlands or peat, or concealed by rocks or sand. Landslides may have buried them, or rivers may have changed course and now flow over them. Some may have been partially destroyed by quarries or gravel-pits, while others may have had factories or office buildings or housing estates built on top of them.

The location and identification of such sites presents a real challenge to the field-archaeologist.

Let us consider some of the tasks which the amateur field-archaeologist can undertake. Here is a list:

1. *Prehistoric remains.* This involves the recognition of different types of burial mounds, settlement sites, field systems and associated monuments.

2. *Roman remains.* Field-work includes the locating of the sites of such structures as Roman villas, signal stations, temples and posting-stations. Tracing the routes of Roman roads is another useful activity, as is the location of Roman industrial sites.

3. *Early medieval.* The location of the sites of early Celtic monasteries. Locating the sites of Norse and Danish houses and settlements. Identifying earthworks of uncertain date, but believed to belong to the 'Dark Ages'. Identifying early Anglo-Saxon settlements, and deserted village sites.

4. *Later periods.* Making a survey of post-Roman roads, including old stage-coach routes. Making a study of the walled towns of Britain. Investigating structures associated with the Civil War, and its battlefields. Making a study of old types of dwellings, such as 'cruck cottages' and 'long houses'.

There are other jobs which need doing, but that is enough to be going on with.

Tasks connected with industrial archaeology will be described later.

All these are jobs which can be conducted by a small group of amateur archaeologists. All that is needed to undertake them is a certain amount of knowledge and experience and some simple equipment. Obviously the suggestions I have listed above include jobs which can be divided into two kinds – the relatively simple ones, which need some knowledge and the capacity for observation, and the harder jobs which call for more profound knowledge and technical skill. One graduates from the simpler jobs to the harder jobs.

Now for the second of those questions to which I said we needed to know the answer before undertaking field-archaeology: *How do we set about recognising sites?* There are several answers to this one. A site may be located:

1. By exposure, either accidental or otherwise, which causes evidence of the hidden site to be shown on the surface of the ground.
2. By evidence mentioned in historical documents.
3. By the study of maps.
4. By the study of place-names.
5. By the study of air-photographs.
6. By local legends and information.
7. By probing for sites.
8. By having an eye for country.

Let's consider these points in more detail.

1. *The discovery of sites by exposure*. The discovery of a site is often due to its being exposed by natural or human agencies – animals, wind or water, farming and building activities.

Rabbits and other creatures burrow into a buried

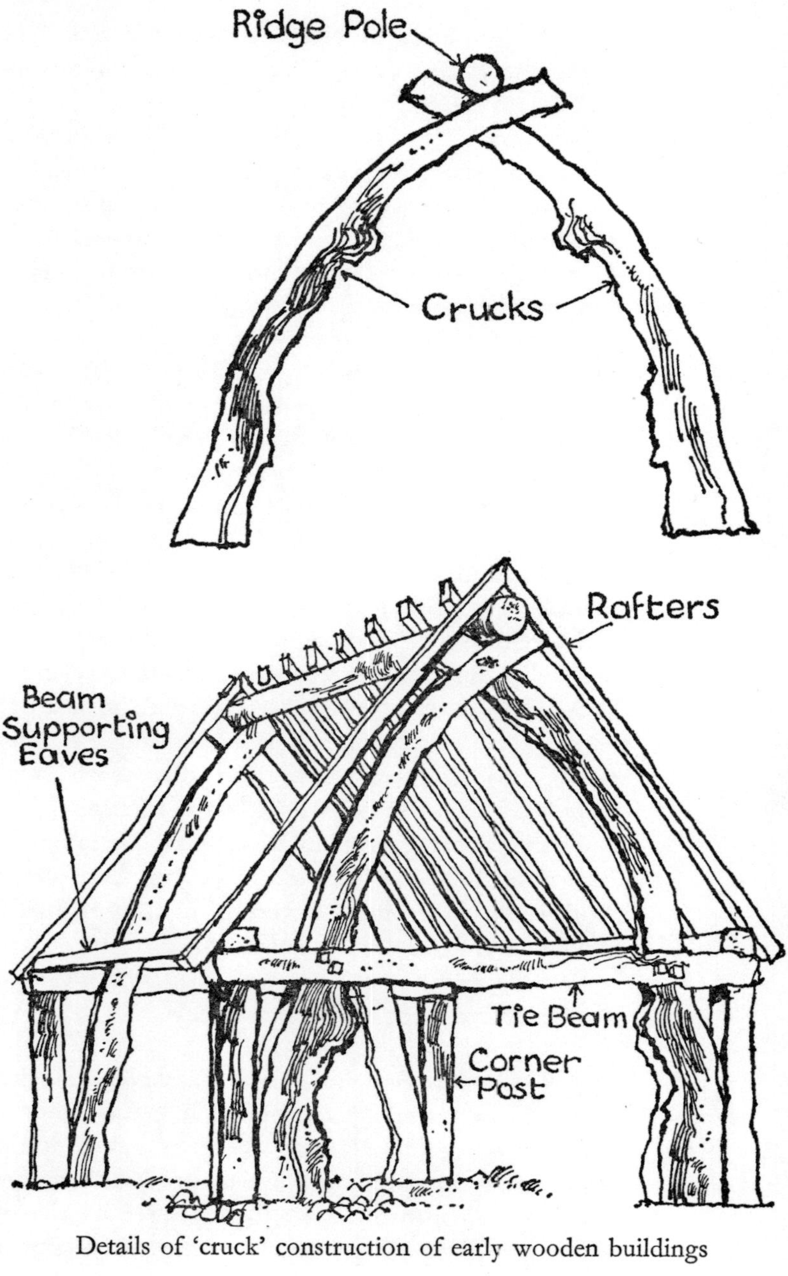

Details of 'cruck' construction of early wooden buildings

structure and bring up bits of pottery, tile, coins. The observant archaeologist will notice these objects and realize that the site is worth investigating.

Wind may blow away sand or soil and expose the hidden building. This happened at the Bronze Age settlement at Skara Brae, in the Orkney Islands, where stone-walled houses were exposed. At Culbin Sands, Morayshire, parts of the sand-buried settlement of Culbin are exposed from time to time.

The movement of water – by river or sea – often exposes buried settlements, fortifications and cemeteries, as cliffs and river-banks are worn away. This is happening all along the British coastline. The east coast of Yorkshire and the Wirral peninsula of Cheshire are two areas where prehistoric and Roman settlements have been exposed and destroyed.

The activities of man have also led to the discovery of many unsuspected archaeological sites. Ploughmen and other farm workers may uncover the remains of buried buildings, roads, cemeteries. Chedworth Roman villa, in Gloucestershire, was discovered by a man digging for a ferret trapped in a rabbit hole. Lullingstone villa, in Kent, was first discovered while somebody was digging post-holes for a fence.

The uncovering by a builder of stone paving under the council houses he was erecting, at Norton, Yorkshire, led to the discovery of a Romano-British town of the Parisi or 'Chariot People'.

Peat-diggings, stone quarries and gravel pits have also produced many unsuspected finds.

2. *The use of historical documents*. Many archaeological sites are discovered by a reference in the writings of earlier investigators. During the past few centuries several generations of writers have produced descriptions of the history and topography of the districts in which they lived. These accounts very often contain

clues to the location of antiquities no longer visible on the ground.

There is almost certain to be at least one such book, and probably more, about the area in which you live. Or there may be a collection of unpublished manuscripts – the work of local investigators – which can be consulted at your local library. There may be a society devoted to the study of local history which can help you.

3. *Map study*. The maps produced by the Ordnance Survey are among the most useful tools available to the archaeologist. No purposeful investigation can be carried out until you have studied the appropriate maps of the district in which you want to work. Maps are invaluable for finding your way about: for learning about sites that have already been discovered; and for recording new finds and sites.

Ordnance Survey maps illustrating the various prehistoric and historic periods in Britain – the Archaeological and Period maps – have already been described. We are concerned here with topographical maps; that is, maps which show the appearance of a piece of country *now* – its natural features, settlements, roads and railways, and other evidence of human activity.

Topographical maps are produced to a variety of scales, from ten miles to one inch to approximately fifty inches to one mile. (Such large scale maps are more properly known as *plans*). There is no point in giving a detailed description of the different types of maps here* since our concern is only with maps of use to the archaeologist.

Three maps are of use to the field-workers – those on the scales of one-inch-to-one-mile, two-and-a-half-

* For a detailed account of different types of maps consult *The Historian's Guide to Ordnance Survey Maps*, published by the National Council of Social Service, 1964.

inches to one mile, and six inches to a mile. The first is useful for finding one's way about, the others for locating particular sites and find-spots. The six-inch map is particularly useful for marking in the sites of new discoveries, with notes of any special details.

The amount of archaeological detail shown on a map varies with the size of the scale. Maps on a scale of one-inch-to-a-mile show most well-known antiquities, especially those open to the public. Prehistoric remains are shown, as well as the sites of vanished villages, as on the Yorkshire Wolds and elsewhere.

The two-and-a-half-inch maps show much more local detail, indicating the sites of such features as vanished manor-houses and earthworks. The six-inch map gives the greatest amount of detail. As well as the major antiquities and sites of structures, the locations of individual finds are indicated, with a note referring to the date of discovery and type of find – e.g. 'Roman coins found, 1868'.

There is room on such a map to write down your own observations and discoveries.

The Ordnance Survey uses different type-faces to indicate different types of antiquities. Archaeological sites are divided into three groups, and each is marked with its own form of lettering.

1. Prehistoric remains. Anything earlier than AD 43 (that is, before the Roman conquest) is lettered in Old English characters; thus, **'earthwork'**.

2. Roman remains, dating from AD 43 to AD 410, are indicated by simple capital letters, such as ROMAN ROAD or ROMAN VILLA.

3. Later antiquities, dating from the end of the Roman period to AD 1688 (the accession of William and Mary), are marked in German text, such as **"Haddon Hall"**.

Such maps, indicating the many different types of antiquities dating from various periods of past history, present a wonderful picture of the appearance of the countryside bequeathed to us by the labours of bygone generations.

I have praised Ordnance Survey maps, but for finding my way about the countryside I use Bartholomew's half-inch contoured maps, a series which covers all Great Britain. These are beautiful maps, coloured to show heights and indicating a considerable amount of archaeological detail. It is worthwhile to have one's own collection of these (the paper editions are cheap enough), as well as the appropriate Ordnance Survey maps.

You probably learned at school how to use the National Grid system for locating a particular place on a map. It is helpful to be able to give the national grid reference numbers for a site, rather than some imprecise directions such as 'three miles north-west of Norton' or 'a hundred yards from the Pig and Whistle'. A grid is a combination of squares designed to facilitate reference to a map, and is now printed on all Ordnance Survey maps.

4. *Place names.* There are said to be 20,000 places in Britain, and the names of many of them give a clue to their origins and history. Some names date back to Norman, Saxon, Scandinavian or Celtic times.

The study of place names is a vast subject, where even experts disagree, but it is useful to read one or two books which explain the principles. *English Place Names* by J. Stokes (Batsford) is a good introduction.

Certain terms indicate that a certain type of antiquity may be found there. A name including the word *wall* or *walls* suggests an old stone structure, perhaps a Roman fort or villa.

Whether or not any actual place-names of Roman origin survive is a matter for experts to decide, but names embodying *chester* or *cester* are still used for towns which developed from Roman settlements. Chester, from the Latin *castra,* a fort, was a word borrowed by the Saxons, and applied by them to any place with stone walls.

Names embodying such terms as 'bury', 'borrow' or 'burg' also imply old fortifications, and are worth investigating. Terms such as 'street', 'stret' or 'strat', forming part of a place-name, are clues to the existence of an old road, perhaps Roman. 'Stan' or 'stane' in a place-name comes from the Saxon for 'stone place'. Monuments from antiquity were also attributed to the Devil, hence such names as the Devil's Dyke, Devil's Arrows, and so on.

The study of place-names is closely linked with map-study and local legends.

5. *Aerial photographs.* There is no finer way of gaining an impression of a piece of countryside than by flying over it. (I still remember the wonder with which I first viewed the mountains and plains of the Isle of Man from the air). But, since this is not often possible, much can be learned from a study of air photographs. To be able to interpret an aerial photograph is as helpful as being able to read a map, for sites which are invisible on the ground may still be visible from the air.

A fact of great importance to the archaeologist is that once a piece of ground has been disturbed – by digging a ditch or hole, or by erecting a building or earthwork – the evidence of that disturbance can never be erased. Ditch and hole may be filled in, and building and earthwork levelled so that no evidence of their existence is visible on the surface. But evidence *does* exist *below* the surface, for the soil which fills the cavity will be of a different colour and texture from that surrounding it. Buried stonework makes its existence known by a difference in the vegetation pattern above it. These things are difficult to observe from ground level, but show up from the air.

Such facts have resulted in many sites being discovered by a study of aerial photographs. On a photograph, vanished sites can be located by three different kinds of clues. They are: (1) Shadow Marks, (2) Crop Marks, (3) Soil Marks.

1. 'Shadow marks' mean that sites are revealed by the shadows cast by almost-vanished earthworks. The banks of an earthwork or field boundary may have been so flattened by ploughing that they are almost indistinguishable on the surface. But at certain times of the day, in early morning or late evening, even such features of low relief cast a shadow. To the observer of the ground these shadows are of no particular significance. But to the observer from the air the shadows will be seen to assume a more or less definite shape – the shape of the vanished structure or enclosure. They show up as a darker pattern. An air photograph will also show the site as a whole, giving meaning to what, viewed at ground level, is a mere jumble of shadows.

Low relief sites can also be used to provide evidence of vanished monuments under certain weather conditions. In winter, driven snow tends to accumulate along the line of banks and earthworks. In periods of heavy rain, water tends to do the same. Something of the outline of the vanished structure is shown.

2. 'Crop marks'. This means that sites can be located by the outline of their walls and ditches which show in varying patterns of vegetation in cornfields and pastures. Plants depend for their growth on the depth of soil and the nourishment it contains. In a field which contains a buried building, the line of the walls will be indicated by rows of stunted plants, since the hidden stonework will have prevented root development. An aerial photograph will show the shape of a

buried building in a field, the outlines of the walls showing as lines of stunted plants or bare patches.

Such outlines show up as lighter coloured markings against the darker coloured crops – wheat, clover and so on.

Conversely, where ditches and pits have been dug and filled in, a greater depth of soil exists, and plants grow taller. Again the pattern of vanished excavations will show up on an aerial photograph.

These techniques depend upon the effect of *contrast,* and are more clearly seen during a hot, dry summer. A period of drought is useful to the archaeologist, for the outlines of hidden walls and ditches are particularly noticeable, owing to the differences between vegetation which is still flourishing and vegetation whose growth is retarded.

Although crop-marks are a useful method of gaining information about a vanished site, care must be taken not to confuse them with remains of modern times which present a similar appearance – farm buildings, drainage ditches, and so on, of recent date. Even the site of a manure heap, seen on an aerial photograph, can be mistaken for a tumulus!

3. 'Soil marks'. This means that sites can still be located by the difference in colouring of soil in a ploughed field. An earthwork, burial mound or building may have been almost completely destroyed, and its remains dispersed across a field by years of ploughing. Yet the materials of which that structure was built will continue to exist in that field for years, appearing as layers of material of a shape and colour different to those of the surrounding soil. Roman buildings have often been discovered because bits of red roofing tiles or coloured mosaic pavements were turned up by the plough.

With some friends I once came upon a man digging a celery trench in a garden and complaining bitterly of the number of stones he encountered. He was very surprised when we told him he was hacking his way through a Roman road!

6. *Local legends.* Country people often possess a considerable amount of knowledge about local sites, particularly about archaeological features which have disappeared. If you talk to them in the right way they will give you much valuable information. Some local stories are of no particular value, but if you listen patiently something of real use may emerge. Experience will teach you to separate fact from fiction.

Local legends, however improbable, often have a basis of truth. I remember, when a boy, being told of a man in golden armour who haunted the road near the town of Mold, in north Wales. When archaeologists excavated a burial mound beside the road they found a man's skeleton complete with golden ornaments. For how many hundreds of years had that story persisted?

7. *Probing for sites.* A circular metal rod a couple of feet long, pointed at one end and with a wooden or metal handle at the other, is an indispensable part of every field-archaeologist's equipment. When walking across a field believed to contain the remains of an old road or building, thrust the metal probe into the ground at intervals of a foot or two. If the probe strikes hard material, this may indicate buried stonework. A succession of such probes will indicate the extent of buried walls, though only a trial trench can prove it. If your probe sinks deep into the soil, then either there is nothing of importance there, or you are off the line of stonework and must start again.

8. *An eye for country.* This term is my own. It is quite unscientific, and cannot be explained logically; yet

every experienced archaeologist would understand what I mean by it. An eye for country is the feeling one gets – a sort of sixth sense – which comes from long experience of tramping across the country looking for evidence of bygone history. You see a long, low earthwork – Roman roads look like that. Or a circular mound – it *might* be the site of an early castle. You have no proof – you don't *know*. But you have this feeling that such a place *should* produce such a site. Further investigation will prove you right or wrong.

The last of my three questions – *What equipment does the field-archaeologist need*? – has really been answered in the course of this chapter. He needs maps, of different scales. A compass, to help in the location of elusive sites. A metal probe. A trowel, for examining exposures of stones and soils. A flat-bladed, diamond-shaped mason's trowel is best. A short pick or trenching tool is useful, too. A measuring-tape for finding the dimensions of earthworks, the 66-foot length being the most useful. A short coiled steel rule, for measuring distances of a yard or so. A ranging-pole, coloured red and white, helps when measuring distances – though a human being will serve this purpose almost as well. A camera to take photographs of sites is a great help, but the photographing of archaeological material differs from ordinary photography, and the advice of some experienced person should be sought. Notebooks and pencils, of course.

And don't forget boots – good, strong boots, which will carry you through mud and water and over rocks and rubble.

Industrial Archaeology

As I pointed out earlier, there is no dividing-line between the study of the remote past – prehistoric, Roman, medieval – and the study of the 18th, 19th and 20th centuries. They are all part of the same long story, and all the proper concern of the archaeologist.

Industrial archaeology is the youngest branch of archaeology. It is little more than fifteen years old: so new, that its methods and fields of research are not yet clearly defined. This gives it great freshness. There is room for newer, younger people, with original ideas. There is scope for pioneers.

Industrial archaeology does not deal with the long-dead past, but with the objects we see all about us today. Factories, workshops, roads, railways, canals, bridges, engines, tools – such things are its concern. It is interested, too, with the men who created these things – inventors, engineers, scientists. It is the study of the physical remains of the industrial civilization created in Britain during the past two centuries. But – an important *but* – it can apply to those remains the techniques which were developed to solve the problems of the older kind of archaeology.

The fact is that we in Britain live amongst the remains of the first great industrial civilisation on this planet. In whatever direction we travel, even on the shortest journey, we cannot avoid meeting with some monument produced by this great civilization. It may be a roadway or a railway, a mill or a furnace, a coalmine or a harbour, or a piece of machinery. Such things we take for granted, until we find they have been destroyed and have vanished for ever. That is happening every day. The civilization of our childhood is replaced as we grow older by another, newer civilization.

I can't better the definition of industrial archaeology given by one of its pioneers, Dr E. R. R. Green. He said it was 'the study of all the monuments left by man in his efforts to control his environment and to create wealth.'

Wealth in this sense doesn't mean gold or money, but all those things man needs to maintain life – farms, workshops, roads, railways, ships, mines. These, with the work-people themselves, are the real wealth of a country.

In order to remain alive we must feed and clothe ourselves and have somewhere to live. To produce food we must clear land and grow crops. To provide ourselves with clothing we must keep sheep to produce wool, or have access to supplies of cotton from abroad. To have a shelter to live in we must know where to get timber, or stone or bricks. To perform all these tasks we must be able to make tools and implements, together in our own day with machinery. Making tools means mining for metal. Transporting the goods we make from place to place implies roadways and railways, as well as means of carrying them – from the pack-horse to the motor-lorry. There must be means of communication. And of course we need a system of orderly government. Together all these objects and activities and achievements add up to make a civilization.

But before men can do such things – grow food, build houses, make clothing and implements, transport people and goods – he must be able to *control his environment*. That is, he must change the countryside in which he lives until it is capable of providing most of the things he needs.

So he cuts down forests, clears land for ploughing. He digs mines and quarries. He extracts stone and clay and metals, and fashions these into buildings to house machines. He harnesses water and wind to provide power. He builds dams across rivers to create water supplies. He constructs roads and canals and railways so that goods and people can move to the places where they are needed. He makes bridges and tunnels to link centres of industry. And only by making changes such as these can human beings create a great industrial civilization.

It is the task of the industrial archaeologist to unravel the story of such activities by investigating the remains left behind. And it is those remains – of buildings, machinery, forms of transportation and so on – that form the subject matter of industrial archaeology.

Now, you can see at once that the industrial archaeologist, unlike his fellow-workers in other branches of archaeology, doesn't normally depend on excavation, on digging up a site. Of course, digging does sometimes come into it, where a structure is ruined or has been buried under a century or so's accumulation of soil. A number of old furnaces, glass-works and pottery-kilns have been recovered in this way. But usually the objects that are studied by the industrial archaeologist are still visible above ground, and his work consists in making a record of a place by means of measurements, drawings, photographs, plans.

Where a structure has endured a long period of disuse or neglect – which has often happened with old mills, workshops and so on – restoration may be involved. Heckington Mill, a few miles out of Boston on the Sleaford Road in Lincolnshire, owes its present magnificent appearance to the activities of the Kesteven County Council who bought it when it had fallen into disrepair and had it restored. Essex County Council has preserved the old mills at Bocking and Upminster. Suffolk County Council has scheduled several windmills for preservation. Such restoration is very like the preservation of older structures such as prehistoric burial mounds, Roman forts or old castles and churches.

A great deal of field-work remains to be done in industrial archaeology. All over the British Isles are the relics of bygone industry. Many of these relics are being destroyed as we watch, to make way for modern factories or power plants or housing estates. If records of such old structures are not made now, then all knowledge of them may be lost as completely as our knowledge of many monuments of prehistory.

Here the amateur can do very useful work. What is involved is visiting and making plans and photographs of buildings, machinery and other features. This investigation can be supplemented by the study of old records: business account books, early trade directories, early newspapers and magazines. Many features of early industry are included in the Ordnance Survey maps of the early 19th century, and searching for these is a fascinating field of study.

'Industrial archaeology, like archaeology in general, can be regarded, according to the ambitions of the person concerned, either as an academic subject, or as an agreeable hobby,' wrote Kenneth Hudson, whose book *Industrial Archaeology* was the first book on the subject for the general reader. 'It can be either a discipline or a pleasure, a means of adding to the world's store of knowledge or a way of increasing one's personal awareness of the past.'

He goes on to point out that industrial archaeology is an essentially practical subject, in which people can expect to be actively and usefully engaged, and one that offers the 'rare satisfaction of being able to work over ground which has not been over-explored already, and where there are real and exciting discoveries still to be made by the sparetime enthusiast.'

What you can do. If this kind of archaeology appeals to you, how can you start learning more about it?

The answer is much the same as with archaeology in general.

1. Join a society.
2. Attend lectures or a training course.
3. Read books and periodicals.
4. Visit as many sites as possible.
5. Take part in field-work.

Joining a society. A number of organizations specialising in industrial archaeology have been founded during recent years in several large towns, and an enquiry at a public library or museum will probably provide you with details. (I'm a member of the Manchester Region Industrial Archaeological Society and have gained much knowledge and experience by attending its meetings and field-trips).

Attending lectures. Again, branches of the Workers' Educational Association and the extra-mural departments of universities arrange lectures and field-trips. Training courses are often held, lasting a week or so, at which one can learn the rudiments of surveying and recording structures and machines.

Reading books and periodicals. Although a new study, industrial archaeology is already developing a literature of its own. I've already mentioned Kenneth Hudson's *Industrial Archaeology: an introduction,* published by John Baker in 1963. Another book useful for beginners is E. R. R. Green's *Introduction to the Industrial Archaeology of the British Isles.* More advanced is J. M. P. Pannell's *Techniques of Industrial Archaeology*; Mr Pannell has also written *Archaeology of Engineering.* A series of regional industrial archaeologies is to be published by David & Charles (Publishers) Ltd, of Newton Abbot, Devon, and will include volumes on Southern England, the

East Midlands, London, Lancashire, Derbyshire, Staffordshire, Shropshire and Wales.

A very fine illustrated book is *The Functional Tradition in Early Industrial Building,* by J. M. Richards. O. G. S. Crawford's *Archaeology in the Field* is well worth reading; and you may find that your local library has a quarterly publication, *The Journal of Industrial Archaeology* (published by David & Charles, Ltd), which contains accounts of recent work in the field.

It's useful to brush up on what they taught you at school about the industrial revolution: J. D. Chambers' *The Workshop of the World* (Oxford, 1961) and T. S. Ashton's *The Industrial Revolution,* 1760–1830 (Oxford, 1948) are first-rate short introductions.

Numerous books deal with one aspect or another of technology. Appearing rather formidable, and 700 pages long, *A Short History of Technology* by T. K. Derry and T. I. Williams (Oxford, 1961) provides a useful dip when you want details of particular topics.

Other useful books are: *The English Windmill,* by R. Wailes (Routledge, 1954); *British Canals,* by C. Hadfield (Macdonald, 1950), and *The Railways of Britain,* by J. Simmons (Routledge, 1961). Enthusiasts for the archaeology of railways will find many Ian Allan publications useful. For vintage car specialists there is *The Veteran and Vintage Magazine* (Pioneer Publications Ltd, 3 Wyndham Place, London, S.W.1). On this subject I have found *The Boys' Book of Veteran Cars,* by E. F. Carter (Burke, 1959), particularly serviceable.

Visiting sites

You should be able to find out, from the books I've recommended or from your local library, the sites connected with industry that are worth a visit in your own area.

It's a good idea to inquire about objects of interest

Donkey working tread-mill, Carisbrooke Castle, Isle of Wight to the industrial archaeologist in the district in which you find yourself spending a holiday. There may be old water- or wind-mills, disused railway lines and stations, collections of motorcars or locomotives.

Or, if you really get hooked, you can deliberately plan a holiday (as I have often done) so that it takes you to all the places of interest within a particular region.

Again, you may have decided to specialize: in canals, perhaps, or old boats or narrow-gauge railways. Industrial archaeology is full of specialists: people who are not so much drawn by the whole field as by some aspect of it that particularly interests them, or is related to some skill of their own in photography, engineering, architecture, building and so on. This situation is deplored by some archaeologists on the grounds that it tends to break the subject into fragments. But there are always people who can put the fragments together.

You might find you were most interested in water and windmills. These are to be found in various counties, though few are now working. Such sources of energy were used for grinding corn, operating circular saws, and driving drills for the boring of cannon. I was surprised to find a watermill still working at Harome, near Kirkby Moorside, East Yorkshire, though it was operated by a water-turbine. At the hamlet of Lowna, a few miles away, was a complete 18th century industrial complex with water mill and tannery.

Windmills are usually more visible than watermills, being sited on high ground. There are good examples in Suffolk – at Woodbridge, Stradbrook, Pettaugh, Syleham and elsewhere. The mill at Saxstead Green is one of the finest. Norfolk has several examples, at Billingford and Paston especially. The mill at Bourn, in Cambridgeshire, dates from the early 17th century and is one of the earliest windmills still standing.

A Wind-Mill

Mr Rex Wailes, who is probably the greatest living authority on windmills, estimates that there may have been as many as 10,000 at work in England at one time.

If you use youth hostels you may have noticed that many of them are housed in old watermills. Scarborough Hostel, in Yorkshire, is one of these; Houghton Mill, near Huntingdon, is another.

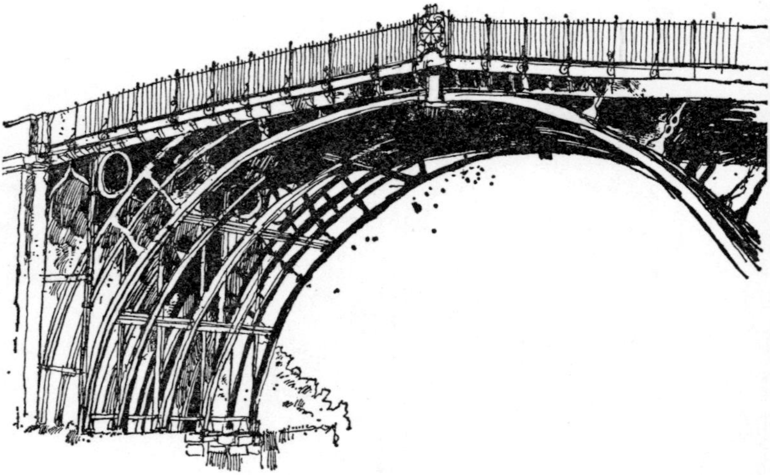

Ironbridge, Shropshire. The oldest iron bridge in the world, dating from 1779

Should your interest be in early industrial plant, you might visit Coalbrookdale in Shropshire, where Abraham Darby's blast-furnace and other 18th century structures associated with an iron foundry still exist, together with an old furnace of 1638. The whole group constitutes one of the most fascinating open air museums in Britain.

Not far away is Ironbridge where, spanning the River Severn and dating from 1779, is the oldest metal bridge in the world.

Abbeydale Industrial Hamlet, comprising an 18th century scythe works and workmen's cottages, has been restored as a monument to the early Sheffield steel industry.

At Styal, near Wilmslow in Cheshire, a cotton-mill of 1784 with its adjoining industrial village can be seen. It is called Quarrybank Mill and in its apprentice house upwards of 200 children lived in the days when child labour was sent to toil in the mills.

In Birmingham a huge engineering workshop has been converted into a Museum of Science and Industry, which displays a whole range of machines, from a beam engine of 1864 to the huge Napier-Railton car in which the late John Cobb established the world land speed record of over 394 m.p.h. in 1947. There is also a scale model of Britain's first atomic pile, made at Harwell in 1948. A silversmith's workshop and a brass foundry have been reconstructed to show typical hand processes in early industry.

An interesting feature of this museum is an actual canal lock (part of the Birmingham and Fazeley Canal), which can be seen from a bridge linking two parts of the building.

If railways are your chief interest then you must visit the Museum of British Transport and the Science Museum, both in London. Don't forget to look at George Stephenson's original locomotive 'The Rocket', on show at the latter building. (To see his first engine, 'Locomotion Number One', you'll have to go to Bank Top Station, Darlington, where it is preserved). Another early locomotive, 'The Invicta', stands by the city wall in Canterbury. Old locomotives are to be found in the most unusual places!

Another place to visit is the Railway Museum at York, housed in the locomotive workshops of the old York and North Midland Railway. This was the first railway museum in the country. The Small Exhibits Section is in the dining-room of the old 1841 railway station. This museum is full of good things, from primitive locomotives such as the one built for Hetton Colliery in 1822, the 'Agenoria' built in 1829 and the 'Columbine' built in 1845.

The Great Western Railway Museum at Swindon contains the world-famous locomotive, 'City of Truro', which reached a record speed of 102 m.p.h. in 1904.

Interesting though museums are, they are not perhaps the most appropriate places for railway engines. Locomotives were meant to move and to be seen in motion. Part of the attraction of rail travel not so long ago were the sights and sounds accompanying the arrival and departure of big steam locomotives – the hiss of the pistons, the clouds of rising steam, the sound of the whistles. Part of that process which I've already discussed, which turns the familiar objects of yesterday into the archaeological objects of today, has been the disappearance of steam locomotion. Now that diesel and electric trains have taken over, a number of railway preservation societies have been founded, forming an important branch of industrial archaeology. Enthusiastic amateurs have laboured with picks and shovels to uncover miles of track buried for years under soil and vegetation. They have scoured the countryside for old locomotives, old carriages, old station and signalling equipment. They have reconstructed railway lines that had been closed or disused for decades. Now, as a result of their efforts, a number of narrow-gauge railways are in working order and are again carrying goods and passengers. Few of these lines have paid staff. Mostly they are run by volunteers, either at week-ends or during holidays.

There are several such resurrected railways in Wales. There is another in Sussex. Others are being reorganised in various parts of the country. The principal ones now in operation include:

1. *The Ffestiniog Railway*. This is the oldest narrow-gauge line in the world that is open to the public.

Map of Railways of England and Wales, about 1860

Started in 1836 to carry slate from the quarries at Ffestiniog, in North Wales, to the harbour at Portmadoc, it was horse-drawn until 1863 when steam took over: one of the original locomotives is still in use. It stopped running in 1946. When a group of enthusiasts began the task of clearing the line in 1954 they found it overgrown with bushes and small trees. It now carries more than 100,000 passengers a year.

2. *The Welshpool and Llanfair Light Railway*. Opened in 1903, closed in 1956, this line runs through the wooded countryside of the Welsh border. Two of the original steam locomotives are still in service.

3. *The Talyllyn Railway*. This connects the seaside resort of Towyn, on the Welsh coast, with the mountain village of Abergynolwyn and Talyllyn Lake at the foot of Cader Idris.

Like the Ffestiniog Railway it was built (in 1865) to carry slate. By 1950 much of the track was in a semi-derelict condition and had to be re-laid by members of a society formed to save the line. The two original locomotives, 'Talyllyn' and 'Dolgoch', have been restored and now haul trains again as they did over a hundred years ago.

4. *The Devil's Bridge Mountain Railway* is the only remaining narrow-gauge line on British Railways. It runs from Aberystwyth up the beautiful Rheidol Valley to the famous beauty-spot of Devil's Bridge.

5. *The Snowdon Mountain Railway*. This has the distinction of attaining a greater height than any other railway in the British Isles. From its terminus at Llanberis, in north Wales, it runs to the summit of Snowdon, 3,560 feet. This is certainly one of the most interesting and exciting train journeys to be made in Britain.

6. *The Bluebell Line*. This Sussex railway was opened in 1882 and closed by British Railways in 1955. Its rolling stock (it was re-opened in 1960) includes several

famous veteran locomotives, among them the Caledonian No. 123, which took part in the great railway race to Aberdeen in 1888. Granada TV restaged 'The Great Train Robbery' on this line. Sheffield Park Station has been restored to its condition in the 1880s, and now serves as a railway museum.

And that reminds me that at Towyn Wharf Station, on the Talyllyn Line, is the Narrow Gauge Railway Museum, containing relics from defunct railways all over Britain.

If you are interested in old railway stations – and they repay study – there are several in our big cities which are worth looking at. Liverpool Road Station in Manchester, built about 1830, is said to be the first passenger station in the world. In Birmingham, Curzon Street Station was the original terminus of the London-Birmingham Railway; it dates from 1838. Temple Meads Station in Bristol was the work of Brunel, the great railway engineer, in 1839–40. Swindon, in Wiltshire, has station buildings dating from 1842, as well as railway workshops of the same period.

There are also a number of fifteen-inch railways, such as the Ravenglass and Eskdale, in the Lake District, and the Hythe and Dymchurch, in Kent, which might more correctly be termed 'miniature railways'.

Railways make one think of bridges – and this country can show a number of outstanding examples. The earliest surviving railway bridge is the Causey Arch built in 1727 to connect a wooden tramway from Tanfield Moor collieries, in Durham, with another tramway leading to coal staithes on the River Tyne. Its designer was a local stone-mason named Ralph Wood. It is no longer in use.

The first iron railway bridge, which carried the Stockton and Darlington Railway over a small stream, was built in 1825. It was replaced by a more modern structure, and is now on show in the York Railway Museum.

During the 19th century a number of magnificent bridges were constructed in various parts of Britain, and are among the finest industrial monuments we possess. If you make a journey of any length to Wales or Scotland you are most likely to encounter one. The High Level Bridge at Newcastle, the Ouse Valley Viaduct in Sussex, the Tay Bridge and the Forth Bridge in Scotland – these are all outstanding examples. The Menai Road Bridge was built in 1826 to link the island of Anglesey to the mainland of Wales, and the Britannia Tubular Bridge of 1850 was constructed to carry the railway over the same strait. The Conway Suspension Bridge, also in North Wales, has the walls and towers of Conway Castle as a background.

For more detail, consult a little book by David Walters, *British Railway Bridges* (Ian Allan).

The Pont Cysylltau Aqueduct on the Shropshire Union Canal is another very impressive industrial monument. The aqueduct crosses the valley of the River Dee four miles east of Llangollen in a series of nineteen stone arches each 121 feet high. A cast iron trough on top of the arches holds the water. The aqueduct was officially opened on November 26, 1805, and records of the event speak with awe of the sight of a long line of boats sailing across the sky.

It might be that your interest lies in other forms of transport – tramways, for instance. The tramcar, like the steam locomotive, is an industrial artifact that within recent times has passed from the scene and become of archaeological interest. It was the first vehicle to provide the mass of our population with cheap transport. These 'street railways' (to use the American term) were once familiar sights in most British towns; but Blackpool, Eastbourne and the Isle of Man are now the only places where tramcars continue to operate.

Although the idea of a passenger-carrying vehicle running on tracks along city streets was an obvious extension of the principle of trains running on tracks from one town to another, it was not until 1860 that the tramcar was introduced into Britain from the United States. The first tramcars were horse-drawn, but in the late 1870s steam was introduced, and in the 1890s electric traction. It is estimated that in the 1920s there were 14,000 tramcars carrying passengers. By the 1950s most of them had disappeared, having been replaced by the present-day diesel-engined bus.

The place to see tramcars is at the Tramway Museum at Crich, in Derbyshire. Don't be put off by that word 'museum', for this is an open-air show. Though the vehicles themselves are housed in buildings which were originally locomotive sheds and workshops used by George Stephenson when he was constructing part of the North Midland Railway, many of the tramcars stand out in the open and you can ride in them along a length of track.

It's like stepping into the past to stand by the track and watch one of these old tramcars coming toward you, to wait for it to stop, to get on board and sit down, to look through the window and see the buildings and people outside. Your ride will take place in a quarry which was opened by George Stephenson to supply limestone for burning in the kilns at Ambergate, a few miles away. It is interesting to know, by the way, that the original railway lines laid down in the quarry by Stephenson, were removed and are now in use on the Talyllyn Railway in north Wales.

Over forty tramcars are on show – horse, steam and electric – brought from all parts of the British Isles and abroad. My favourite is Oporto No. 9, one of the oldest and longest-serving trams in the world. It dates from 1873. It was built in Britain by the Starbuck Car and Waggon Company and shipped out to Portugal. At first it was hauled by six mules, later by steam and electric power. It kept its old wooden seats because sardine-fishery workers might have left an aroma on more expensive upholstered ones.

There is also an odd-looking little steam engine called 'John Bull', dating from 1885, which is one of the most powerful ever built in Britain.

That all these relics are preserved and exhibited here for public inspection is owed to the activities of a group of enthusiasts who formed themselves into the Tramway Museum Society in 1955. They obtained a lease of the quarry, toured the countryside for specimens of this discarded form of transport, brought them to Crich and learned how to preserve them. Members give their services free and are dependent on voluntary contributions. One of their latest acquisitions arrived in dramatic circumstances in August, 1968: a Czech tramcar, restored to the state of splendour in which 50 years ago it used to travel the streets of Prague; the tramcar left its home city a few hours before the Russian invasion, and arrived safely in England nearly a week later.

The distinction between tramways and light railways is a slight one, so I should mention the Manx Electric Railway which carries passengers to the top of Snaefell Mountain, the highest on the Isle of Man. That's 2,034 feet.

But you can no longer enjoy a ride on the first electric tramway system in the British Isles – the Giant's Causeway Tramway in Northern Ireland – for it is now closed. Some of the rolling stock is displayed in the Transport Museum in Belfast, well worth a visit.

A Scottish Tramway Museum Society was formed in 1951 with its headquarters in Glasgow. There is also a Light Railway Transport League, with an address in

London, for persons interested in tramways. It's not worthwhile to include addresses here, for they change and get out of date. Ask your local society, or library.

Motor-car fans are well catered for. Over a hundred old cars are displayed in the Montagu Motor Museum at Beaulieu in Hampshire. It is worth making a special effort to visit this. (Orthodox archaeologists will also find the ruined abbey and Palace House of interest). There is another Motor Museum at Brighton. More old cars are on show in the Transport Museum in Hull (with coaches, tramcars and bicycles), and at the Museum of Transport in Glasgow. The emphasis here is on Scottish motor production from the early days to the present.

Old motor-cars, like old locomotives, turn up in the most unexpected places. Many museums seem to exhibit a few examples. So keep your eyes open.

Worth mentioning are several excellent publications by British Railways and the British Transport Commission. The former sells a little book called *Transport Preserved* which is a good short survey of locomotives, carriages, tramcars, omnibuses and early steamships. It tells about exhibits in the Museum of British Transport, in London. Another useful little publication is *The Steam Locomotive,* describing the work of eight great locomotive engineers. The British Transport Commission has produced *The Horse Bus As A Vehicle* and *Transport Pleasures,* which describes railways, stations, tramways, ships, docks and inland waterways. The four booklets will cost you less than ten shillings.

The omnibus would form an interesting study – its history began in 1829 when George Shillibeer introduced into London this new kind of horse-drawn vehicle for the transportation of passengers. This is a field you might care to explore for yourself.

Water transport appeals to many of us, and we cannot see barges or other craft passing along a river or a canal without wondering where they came from and where they are going to, and what kind of cargoes they are carrying.

It is hard to imagine the British landscape without railways or modern roads and with mainly rivers and canals for the transportation of goods and passengers. Yet that was the situation a hundred and fifty years ago. The countryside was criss-crossed with a system

The Waterways Museum, Stoke Bruerne, Northamptonshire

of natural and man-made waterways along which passed horse-drawn and wind-propelled boats of varied types, transporting cargoes from place to place.

With the growth of the British railway system the canals became disused. Goods and passengers were carried by railway. Yet hundreds of miles of waterways still remain open, and cargo-carrying canal and river craft still operate along them. Something of the atmosphere of the old days, when gaily-decorated boats travelled endlessly along the system of canals, can be sampled still in isolated canalside communities, as at Stoke Bruerne, seven miles from Northampton. The Waterways Museum there is unusual, and its very readable *Handbook* (produced by the British Waterways Board) gives a short account of the history of the canals and of the kind of life that was led by canal people.

In London you are able to travel along the Regent's Canal in the traditionally painted 'narrow boat' *Jason*, passing through a tunnel under the Edgware Road, through Regent's Park and the Zoological Gardens to Camden Town Locks, and returning to 'Little Venice'. The embarkation point is the Canaletto Gallery, Bloomfield Street, W.9.

Worsley canal basin and warehouses, near Manchester, also gives some impression of these waterways as they were a century and more ago. The Bridgewater Canal, seen here, was one of the first in England, and was opened in 1761 to convey coal from the Duke of Bridgewater's mines to Manchester, eight miles away.

Shardlow, by the River Trent, with its wharves and three-storeyed warehouse with wide arch under which boats could run to unload is another monument to the canal era. Read *Narrow Boat* by L. T. C. Rolt, which describes a journey across England in such a craft.

There are many other fascinating canal scenes to be encountered in different parts of the country. Keep your eyes open for them.

A different kind of canal (if you happen to be in Kent) is the Royal Military Canal. This was constructed in the days when this country was fighting Napoleon and an invasion of England by the French army was expected. With its gun-sites and fortified towers the Military Canal was an important part of England's defence system. But it was never used and today is a favourite resort of anglers.

In various ports and harbours round the coasts of Britain other ships are preserved – I wish somebody would make a list of them. I've explored the 'Cutty Sark', at Greenwich, and the 'Victory' at Portsmouth.

Then there is the old paddle-steamer 'Medway Queen' which can be seen in the River Medina, on the Isle of Wight. There must be others.

I must mention that very ancient form of boat – the coracle. It consists of a wickerwork frame covered with canvas. You can still see a few of them on the River Teifi, in Cardiganshire, where they are used by the salmon fishermen. Some archaeologists believe they date back to Neolithic times.

Then there's the curragh, the traditional Irish fishing boat which is still a common sight off the west coast of Ireland, especially around the Aran Islands in Galway Bay. Tarred canvas has now replaced animal skins as a covering for the light wickerwork frames. A voyage in one of these craft is really thrilling.

But this has taken us all the way back from the 20th century to prehistory.

Museums. Museums are not to everybody's liking, but it is thanks to the efforts of their staffs that we possess so many objects connected with the past activities of mankind to help us solve the problems of archaeology. Without museums, much of this wealth of machinery, vehicles, tools and equipment, would have been discarded and destroyed. And the old idea of a museum is changing, from being a place where exhibits are shown by themselves in glass show-cases, to a place where objects associated with a particular period are grouped together as they would have been when in use – so that we get 'period rooms' and 'reconstructions' of workshops and industries. The Geffrye Museum in London is a good specimen of the modern museum, with its Elizabethan Room, Stuart Room, William and Mary Room, and so on. The Castle Museum in York, housed in an old debtors' prison, has gone one better and re-created full-scale streets of shops, dating from Georgian to Edwardian times. We do not look at exhibits in glass cases – we walk amongst them as if we were actually there in time.

Winter months when the weather is bad and we can't do field-work out of doors is the time for visiting museums, though it's always worthwhile to visit the local museum wherever you may be. You never know what you may find.

A few more museums worth visiting include:

Blaise Castle Folk Museum, Bristol, which exhibits, among other things, a reconstructed corn-mill and dairy.

The Museum of Carriages, Maidstone, devoted to the history of horse transport and coach building.

The Yieldingtree Railway Museum, Weston-super-Mare, Somerset contains various types of railway equipment.

The Shuttleworth Collection at Old Warden Aerodrome, Bedfordshire, houses specimens of historical types of aeroplanes, cars, carriages and bicycles.

The Welsh Folk Museum, at St Fagans, four miles west of Cardiff, contains a number of re-erected exhibits, including a woollen factory of about 1760, which is still driven by a water-wheel and produces quilts, rugs, and cloth of traditional Welsh patterns.

The West Yorkshire Folk Museum, Halifax, where, surrounding a cobbled courtyard, are reconstructed workshops, shops, a public house and a cottage.

Working in the field. The task of leaving a record for our descendants of the industrial civilisation of our time and of the past two and a half centuries cannot be done by professional archaeologists. There aren't enough of them; there isn't enough money. It will be done by amateurs, working in their free time, learning the correct techniques, spending their own money.

What contribution can you make to industrial archaeology?

The tasks that need to be done include the examining and recording of machinery; the recording of industrial buildings; the investigation of various forms of power plant; the tracing of post-Roman roads and early railways; the study of particular industries and processes; the restoration and preservation of outstanding examples of buildings such as watermills and windmills, early factories and workshops.

So practical work in industrial archaeology can take many forms, depending on the investigator's special interest. Some fields of study certainly need more highly specialised knowledge than others, and probably have to be left to the experts. The development of engines and machinery requires a considerable knowledge of engineering and mechanics; the development of factories and mills calls for some grasp of building and surveying techniques. But any field (or almost any) – even such fairly complex ones as the growth of particular industries – can be approached by any serious investigator willing to learn.

Some tasks can be carried on by an individual working alone, or with a colleague or two. Tracing disused railways or roads is an example. Others call for a team. To make an adequate record of a big structure such as a cotton-mill or an engineering works requires the co-operation of a number of people, each with his own skill. Measurements have to be made of the various floors and rooms, the building materials have to be examined, photographs taken and plans made. A study of the way the work people lived is important, too, and this requires an interest in human beings and their way of living as much as any particular technical skill.

On a training course organised by the extra-mural department of Manchester University, a group of us were given the task of recording some of the features of a big disused cotton mill in Stockport. 'Mr Orrell's great mill' – as it was described in old records – dated from 1835. No longer a textile mill, it was used as storage space by a local supermarket: they occupied the ground floor, and the rest of the great building, several storeys high, was empty and silent, the haunt of bats and rats.

We made a record of part of the structure, with measuring tapes, cameras, notebooks. Some of us were more interested in the rows of terraced houses grouped about the mill, a memorial to the industrial community that had grown up round it in the early 19th century.

Another field-trip (organised by the Manchester Industrial Archaeological Society) was to examine a big cotton mill at Low Moor, beside the River Ribble near Clitheroe, Lancashire. This was a fine example of an iron-framed, multi-storeyed 19th-century mill. The original building dated from about 1786, but had been rebuilt and enlarged between 1815 and 1830. A thousand workers had been employed there. The place was now semi-derelict, the ground floor used as storage space for cement.

We climbed upward from one floor to another, passing typical spinning floors with cast iron pillars. The mill had combined spinning and weaving, before these two processes became separated. Little was left of the first power plant, a waterwheel and outflow, but the big 19th-century engine-house was in good condition, though now empty. After examining the sites of the early gasometers and gas-house we walked upstream to view the weir and mill-race, long disused.

The mill had last been worked about 1930. A memorial stone recorded that the building had been used as barrack accommodation by the Royal Engineers during the Second World War. Windows were still covered with wartime blackout material.

Low Moor Mill had been more than just a factory. It had been a community as well, and the cottages which housed the workers remained. There were rows of them, two rooms up and two down, constructed back-to-back. We noted the National School of 1846, the early Methodist chapel, the Anglican church.

But what had life been like there more than a hundred years ago?

James Ward, a workman, recorded in his diary facts about early trade unions and the difficulties of the workers in the 'cotton famine' of the 1860s. His diary had been rescued from a rubbish heap where it had been discarded.

Details of these two mills, and many other structures, have been recorded for the National Survey of Industrial Monuments, which is being undertaken by the Council for British Archaeology in collaboration with the Ministry of Works. Details of each structure are entered on a standard record card, with photograph or plan, and the cards are then sent to the Ministry's consultant in Industrial Archaeology. This officer sees that the cards are copied, and indexed and placed in the national collection. The original cards are returned to the local group of workers to be included in their own collection.

What other types of jobs are there waiting to be done?

What about helping to make a survey of surviving beam-engines?

What about making a study of roads of post-Roman date, since little work seems to have been done?

What about making a survey of a particular industrial area of a big city, such as the Ancoats district of Manchester, or the 'Gun Quarter' of Birmingham?

Keen field-archaeologists will discover many more possibilities.

I'll end with a quotation from Professor Jack Simmons:

'Since Layard worked at Nineveh and Schliemann at Troy, archaeology has wrought wonders in revealing to us the hidden life of men in the past. Its methods and techniques have much that is valuable to offer us – in addition to the enjoyment that personal envolvement gives – in the pursuit of our own industrial history.'

Some Potted Archaeology

This section consists mainly of facts. These facts are basic knowledge which the beginner needs to know if he or she is to derive the most benefit from viewing archaeological remains. You'll pick up most of the facts as you go along, but it may be useful to have them here in tabulated form.

Many people are familiar (vaguely, at any rate) with the terms used to describe the peoples who lived in Britain before us – the Palaeolithic or Old Stone Age, the Mesolithic or Middle Stone Age, the Neolithic or New Stone Age, and then the Bronze Age and the Iron Age. These are merely convenient labels for peoples whose real names we do not know. After them came the Romans, the Anglo-Saxons, the Scandinavian peoples – Danes and Norsemen – and the Normans. Details of how these different peoples lived can be found in other books; our main concern here is with the remains of one sort or another which they have left behind.

There are a number of concepts and technical terms, some of which are difficult to grasp. The first one is:

Time Scales. It is hard to realize the long periods of time involved where history and prehistory are concerned, so here are three time-scales to show the relative lengths of the periods of time with which archaeologists have to deal.*

Scale 1. This shows the insignificant length of time

* Reprinted from: *Field Archaeology: Some Notes for Beginners*, published by the Ordnance Survey (H.M.S.O. 1963), with the sanction of the Controller of Her Majesty's Stationery Office.

from the New Stone Age to modern times, in comparison with the half million years or so since man first appeared in Britain. Britain was not then an island.

Scale 2. This shows the relative lengths of the main periods of human development since the close of the last Ice Age, round about 12,000 BC. Britain's later

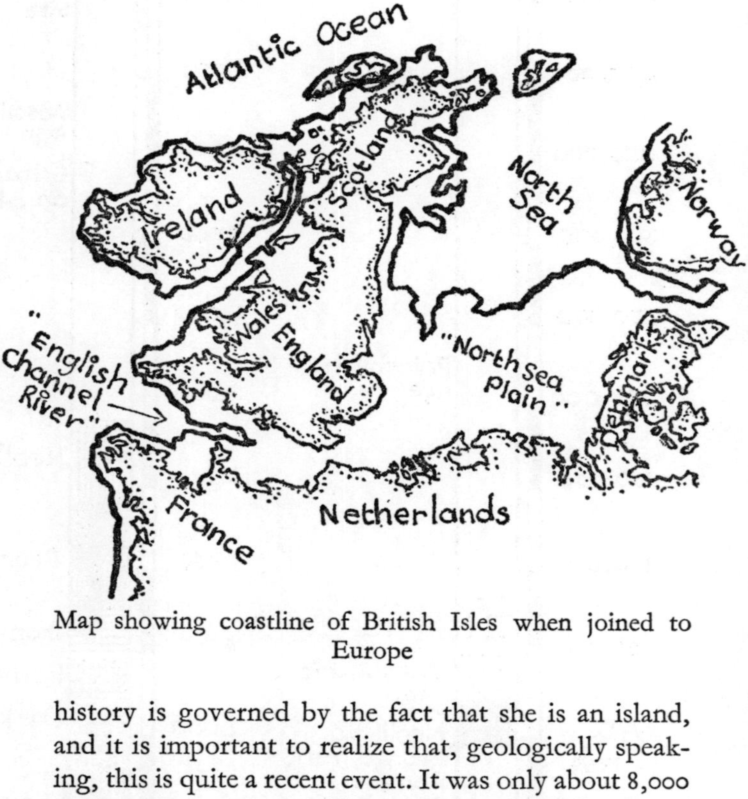

Map showing coastline of British Isles when joined to Europe

history is governed by the fact that she is an island, and it is important to realize that, geologically speaking, this is quite a recent event. It was only about 8,000 years ago that the land-bridge joining Britain to the Continent was finally cut through by the sea, and Britain became an island.

Scale 3. This attempts a more detailed sub-division of the period from the end of the Mesolithic or Middle Stone Age to the present day, with the relative

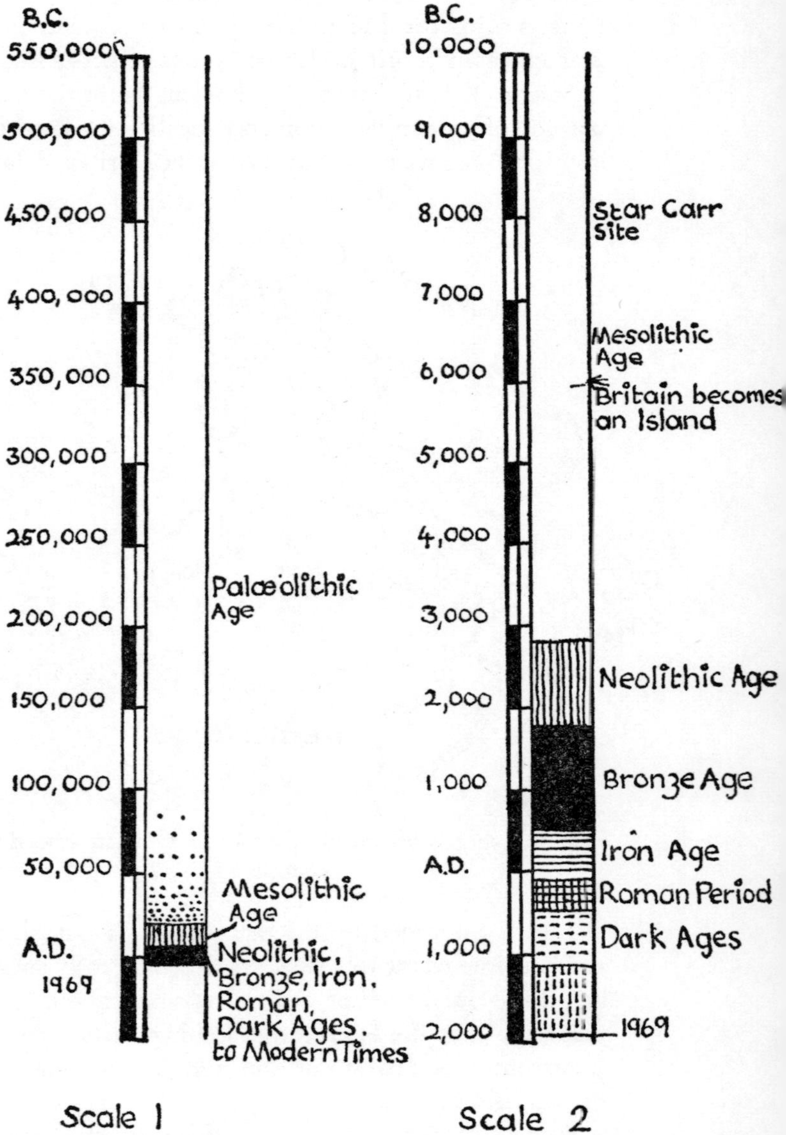

Time Scales to show the comparative lengths of time since the first appearance of Man in Britain and the ending of the last Ice Age.

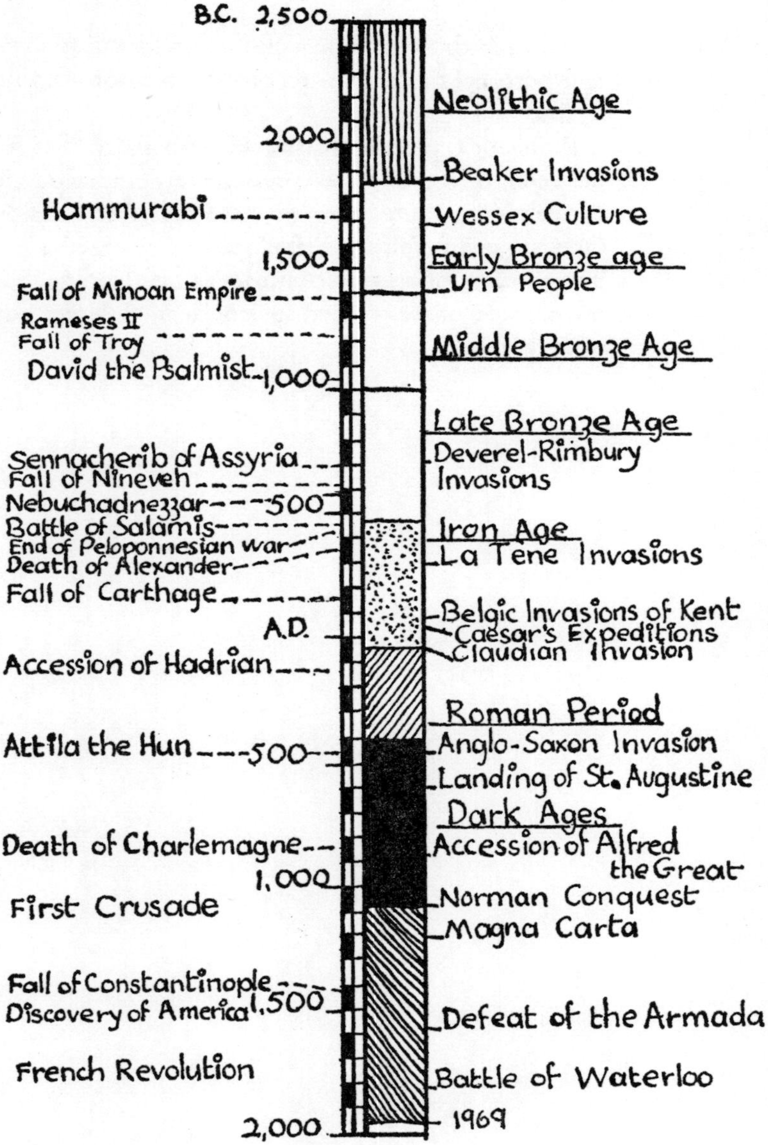

Scale 3

Time Scale to show the relative positions in Time of some well-known events and persons. (*Reprinted with the sanction of the Controller of Her Majesty's Stationery Office*) position in time of some well-known historical events and personalities shown to give its relation to world affairs.

Prehistoric phases are shown with sharp divisions between them, but these are merely archaeological conventions; there were no hard and fast divisions. One stage of cultural development changed slowly into another, often with centuries of overlapping. Such transitional phases varied in length in different parts of Britain.

Some Terms Used in Archaeology

Artifact An object made by man as opposed to something shaped by the forces of nature.

Barrow (or *Tumulus*) A burial mound of earth or stone.

Beacon A hill or structure from which a warning or a message could be despatched by smoke-signals.

Beaker People The first Bronze Age settlers were thus labelled by archaeologists, after the characteristic type of pottery found in their graves.

Belgae An Iron Age people who migrated to Britain from the Continent in the first century BC.

Bell-pit An early type of mine shaft, narrower at the mouth than the bottom.

Berm The level strip of ground between a rampart and a ditch.

Bole Hill A hilltop where the prevailing wind could be used to help smelt lead ore in primitive furnaces.

Black-and-White Building An old building with a framework of oak beams, and the wall spaces filled with plastered lathes or brickwork. (Also known as 'magpie houses').

Broch A circular stone tower used as a fortified residence by Iron Age families in Scotland.

Burin A type of flint tool.

Cairn A mound of stones.

Cashel A type of fort enclosed within a stone wall, found in Ireland.

Celt Bronze or stone chisel-edged prehistoric implement. (Pronounced with a soft 'c' when used in this sense).

Celt A general label for groups of peoples from the

Continent who were occupying the British Isles at the time of the Roman invasion. (The 'Ancient Britons' of old history books).

Culture A stage in the development of the equipment of a group of people in which all their artifacts show a similarity and relationship, so that they can be recognized and identified wherever they may be found.

Cromlech (or *Dolmen*) A box-like tomb, often looking like a big stone table, of the type termed *megalithic*.

Cruck House A building with a framework of pairs of timbers, each pair being cut from a single tree and forming a series of arches.

Cup Mark A slight hollow sunk in the face of stone slabs and associated with megalithic structures. Probably of religious significance.

Deserted Villages Villages which were abandoned or destroyed several centuries ago, and the outlines of whose houses and gardens can be seen under the turf in many parts of the country.

Dun A fort similar to a cashel. Found in Scotland and Ireland.

Dewponds Shallow pools to collect rainwater, made by farmers in districts where there was little surface water.

Ecology The study of the relationship between a living organism and its environment – soil, vegetation, climate, etc. Archaeology is an aspect of human ecology.

Enclosure Roads Roads constructed in the 18th and 19th centuries when the big open fields of medieval times were converted into individual farms.

Figurine A small stone or clay figure which may have been used as a charm or mascot, often with pronounced features indicating fertility.

Fosse A ditch. (The Fosse Way was a Roman road running from Lincoln to Exeter).

Food Vessel Early Bronze Age people named after the typical pottery found in their graves.

Glass House A structure dating from the 16th and 17th centuries where glass-making was carried on. The remains are often found in old woodland districts.

Green Road The grass-covered remains of an old road, which may date from Roman or medieval times. (Also known as 'drove roads' because cattle were driven along them to the market towns).

Grim The Anglo-Saxons often applied the name of Grim to earthworks and other structures made by people who had lived in Britain before them – thus, Grim's Ditch, Grims-pound, Grimsbury, etc. Grim was another name for Woden, the chief god of the pagan Anglo-Saxons.

Henge A type of prehistoric structure consisting of a circular ditch and bank, with one or more entrances, used for religious ceremonies. Sometimes a circle of stone stood inside. Stonehenge and Avebury are two outstanding examples.

Hollow Way A sunken road or track with banks rising steeply on either side. Some may date back to the Bronze Age.

Hypocaust A form of central heating used in Roman times by means of which hot air was circulated under the floors of rooms. The heat came from a furnace. The remains of the hypocaust system are often the only part of a villa which survive.

Inclined Plane A sloping hillside up which small canal boats were conveyed on wheeled bogies on rails, from the lower level of a canal to a higher level. Used where locks were considered impracticable.

Long House An early type of house in which the family lived at one end, and the cattle at the other. A number of these old houses survive in Wales, Yorkshire, and elsewhere, though nowadays the cattle are housed in a separate building, and what was formerly their end of the building is now converted into a dairy, or kitchen.

Lynchet Where a hillside has been ploughed down the slope for a number of years, the soil tends to slide downhill and collect in the form of a sloping platform.

Megalithic A term applied to structures built with big stones. Stonehenge is a typical example.

Mesolithic The Middle Stone Age, which began about 10,000 BC, until 3,000 BC. It marks the last phase of the hunting and food-gathering cultures.

Menhir A tall, upright standing stone.

Microlith Very small flint tools used by Mesolithic peoples. They are small flakes about an inch long, carefully chipped and shaped.

Motte A conical mound with a flat top on which early Norman castles were built.

Neolithic The New Stone Age, dating from perhaps 3,000 BC to 1,800 BC.

Neotechnic A term invented by Lewis Mumford to describe the later stages of our present-day machine-dominated civilization.

Open Fields The system of very large fields surrounding farming settlements which existed before it was replaced in the 18th century by the modern system of relatively small fields.

Ogham A form of writing used in Britain and Ireland about the 6th century AD.

Palaeolithic The Old Stone Age, the first million years or so of man's life on Earth, until about 12,000 BC.

Palaeotechnic Lewis Mumford's term to describe the early stages in the development of our present industrial civilization.

Patina An encrustation on flint and bronze implements.

Pict or Pictish The Picts may have been a fusion of Celtic and Bronze Age peoples, living in Scotland.

Quern A stone hand-mill for grinding corn.

Rake A term used by lead miners to indicate a fissure which was once filled with ore.

Rescue Dig An archaeological excavation undertaken because the site will presently be destroyed by the erection of buildings or some similar undertaking, and it is necessary to gain as much information as possible before this happens.

Ridge-and-Furrow Old patterns of ploughing which appear in fields as alternate strips of ploughed land separated by shallow ditches. Often associated with deserted village sites.

Runes A type of early alphabet used by the Anglo-Saxons and Scandinavians.

Salt Road A route followed by salt-merchants and their pack trains to carry salt from the workings to the market towns.

Toll House A small building, often octagonal or hexagonal, projecting into a road, where tolls were collected from travellers and vehicles in the late 17th and 18th centuries.

Toot Hill High places from which men tooted or kept watch in times of danger.

Zones Geographically Britain is divided into a high-land and land zone and a lowland zone, each having its particular type of archaeological remains.

Learn From Books

No one book will contain all the information you require, so here are details of a number I have found useful. Many can be bought in paperback editions for a few shillings.

A useful introduction to life in Britain, up to Saxon times, is *Going Into the Past,* by G. J. Copley (Penguins). *Four Thousand Years Ago,* by G. Bibby (Penguins) gives a vivid picture of life in Britain and Europe in prehistoric times. Professor G. Childe's *What Happened in History* (Penguins) describes man's technical development.

L. Cotterell's *The Great Invasion* (Pan Books) is an introduction to the study of Roman Britain, as is his *Seeing Roman Britain* (Pan). *Roman Britain,* by I. A. Richmond (Penguin) contains much basic information. A vivid account of life in Roman times is contained in *The Grandeur That Was Rome,* by J. C. Stobart (Four Square Books).

The Vikings, by J. Brøndsted (Penguin) is an excellent account of these seafarers.

Alan Sorrell's illustrated *Living History* (Batsford) is a fascinating book describing archaeological remains from the Stone Age to Tudor coastal forts.

There are many other useful books, dealing with castles, churches, monasteries, houses – ask your librarian about them.

Archaeology is a world-wide subject, so read *The Treasures of Time,* by Leo Deuel (Pan Books) which contains first-hand accounts of great archaeological investigations. G. Bibby's *The Testimony of the Spade*

(Fontana) must not be missed. Leonard Cotterell has written a number of books of great archaeological interest – *The Wonders of Antiquity, Lost Cities, The Enemy of Rome* – all worth reading. He edited the *Concise Encyclopaedia of Archaeology* (Hutchinson) which is useful for looking up details of discoveries and techniques. *The Walls of Jericho,* by M. Wheeler (Arrow Books) is amusing and instructive.

For methods and techniques, *Archaeology and Society,* by G. Clark (Methuen) and *A Short Introduction to Archaeology,* by G. Childe (Muller) are both good introductions. *Approach to Archaeology,* by Stuart Piggott (Penguin) is written for the serious student.

In a class by itself is *Field Archaeology: Some Notes for Beginners,* published by the Ordnance Survey. Several generations of amateur archaeologists have been brought up on this publication, which has now reached its fourth edition.

Periodicals. Antiquity, edited by Dr G. Daniel, which will keep you up to date. A new publication, *Current Archaeology,* published by A. & W. Selkirk, from 128 Barnsbury Road, London, N.W.1 is just the thing for the amateur who wishes to increase his knowledge.

And don't forget the *Illustrated London News* – there are always articles and photographs of archaeological interest. Most libraries can get copies.

Index